To J[...]

May Gods richest blessings
rest on you
Numbers 6:24-26

From Despair To Deliverance

KATHARINE SYLVESTER

Katharine Sylvester

WINEPRESS WP PUBLISHING

Printed in the United States of America

Packaged by WinePress Publishing, PO Box 428, Enumclaw, WA 98022. The views expressed or implied in this work do not necessarily reflect those of WinePress Publishing. Ultimate design, content, and editorial accuracy of this work are the responsibilities of the author.

Unless otherwise noted all scriptures are taken from the Holy Bible, New International Version, Copyright © 1973, 1978, 1984 by the International Bible Society. Used by permission of Zondervan Publishing House. The "NIV" and "New International Version" trademarks are registered in the United States Patent and Trademark Office by International Bible Society.

ISBN 1-57921-224-7
Library of Congress Catalog Card Number: 99-64540

Acknowledgments

I want to thank my husband Hubert and my brothers and sisters for encouraging me to continue with the process of recording the history of our family.

I want to especially thank Mr. Alex Lichtenstein for his encouragement and for his very capable editing of this manuscript. He has given unselfishly and devotedly to this monumental task.

My husband and I deeply appreciate the excellent work that he has done to make this publication possible.

I want to dedicate this book to my parents, Heinrich and Anna Rogalsky, who are now both in the presence of the Lord, for taking the risk to leave Russia in those critical times and to come to the United States without any assurances to give us the opportunity of freedom.

Editor's Note

I have had the privilege of knowing Katharine Rogalsky Sylvester for a number of years. During those years, Katharine and her husband Hubert have become very close personal friends of mine, so when Katharine informed me of her desire to create this history, I was delighted.

Katharine has worked very hard over the past several years compiling this information—recreating a history of her family's arduous journey out of oppressive Russia—and her work has rendered this fine publication. It is one that she should be very proud of. Personally, I am very proud of her for putting this together, and it has be an incredible privilege to me to participate in the editing of her manuscripts. The process has been a long and fruitful journey that I am happy to have been a part of.

In addition to the incredible journey of her family, this work has offered to me a new knowledge of the roots, history, and of the struggles of the Mennonites. I hope that all readers find this work as interesting and inspiring as I have.

ALEX LICHTENSTEIN
Friend and Editor

Introduction

Let me explain the purpose of writing this document and how it has come about. While I was attending The Bible Institute of Los Angeles in the years 1943-1946, I was given the opportunity to share my Christian testimony many times. As I was sharing about the grace of God in my life, I was told, so many times, "You must record this so we can read and remember how God has dealt in your life."

As I was growing up it was difficult to record incidents, and I did not realize the impact that God would have in my life. As a result, I have not remembered all that I would like to, so I took the liberty of taking my mother on a trip to visit my youngest daughter and her new family in 1985. I questioned my mother the entire 2000 miles and recorded on tape all that she could remember about her history, the history of my father, and my own early beginning in life. I also have read extensively several books of the history of my heritage and have made an effort to incorporate that material with my memory to make sense of the cultural differences in my early childhood.

My uncle, John Block, did a great deal of research on our travels and of the early history of our Mennonite background. With his permission, I am using the technical, historical background to provide a basis on how we came to be in Russia, why we left, and all that happened during that time in our lives. In so doing, I have been reminded so often how God told Moses, Joshua, and other Old Testament patriarchs to make altars and to tell the people how God had delivered them from the bondage of Egypt—to tell the children lest they forget what God has done.

> Deuteronomy 5:15; "Remember that you were slaves in Egypt and that the Lord your God brought you out there with a mighty hand and an outstretched arm."

> Deuteronomy 4:9 "Only be careful, and watch yourselves closely so that you do not forget the things your eyes have seen or let them slip from your heart as long as you live. Teach them to your children and to their children after them."

It is with this purpose in mind, that I write to tell the mystery of the grace of God in my life and my extended family. To all that are interested in the faithfulness of God, I write so that He will receive all the glory and praise and honor in His dealings in our lives and my life specifically. Many times, I heard my uncles and grandparents compare our journey from Russia to the United States to that of the journey of Israel from Egyptian bondage to the Promised

Land. So, you may liken this testimony to my personal spiritual journey.

I want my children not to forget the faithfulness of God and I want my siblings not to forget what God has done in our lives. The marvelous grace granted by Him to bring us to a land of freedom so that we could experience the grace of God in our lives. I have been touched and reminded so often in recent days that, except for the Grace of God, we would still be in bondage and poverty in Russia. Yet, here we are in free America with the blessings of knowing God and experiencing His love and mercy in a rich and wonderful way.

There are nine children in my mother's and father's family: I, Katharine Sylvester, am the oldest; Helen Pauls; Anna Simon; Mary Nickel; Henry Rogalsky; Frank Rogalsky; John Rogalsky; Peter Rogalsky; and David Nick Rogalsky. We are all living and in California. We are all married with children and we are all successful. That in itself tells a lot about my parents.

In 1978 I was able to make a return trip to Russia with my uncle, Jacob Block, and his wife, Elizabeth, my uncle, John Block, and my sister, Ann Simon, to revisit relatives who had been left behind and to see what God had delivered us from. It was a trip into my heritage and was a very emotional trip for me. I shall always be grateful for that unique experience. For that reason, I want to record my knowledge of our history so that our children will remember the Godly heritage they have and be grateful for the price their ancestors paid for their freedom.

Each of us has a story to tell and each of our stories are different. This is the account of how God has led and directed in my family and my life.

Russia the Land of Opportunity

John Block is my uncle. His history and research are used with his permission. In addition, just prior to her death, I interviewed my mother in considerable detail to write this family story.

In order to make events understandable they must be placed in historical perspective. Therefore, I must go back earlier in history than our history. In fact, I need to go back to the time of the reformation in the 1520's. Most of us are familiar with the best-known reformers. Martin Luther is the well-known reformer in Germany.

In 1531 Meno Simon was an ordained Catholic priest of Newwarden Friesland, North Holland. As a result of his study, he concluded that those brethren were properly interpreting the Scriptures and he left the priesthood and was baptized as a new believer. He became the foremost spokesman for the Anabaptist movement. Those brethren became followers of Meno Simon and later came to be known as Mennonites.

The Mennonites were persecuted nearly every place they went and finally they settled near the Polish border in Danzig in northern Germany. They were convinced by the Scriptures that they could not take human life and therefore refused to participate in the military. Because of their industriousness, they were accepted in Prussia. It was here that their language of Flemish and Friesish Dutch dialects changed in the late 16th century to "Low German." In Prussia, they remained a separatist group because of their religious differences. They did not live in communes, but they developed a strong community bond as part of their ethnic identification.

Catherine II the Great lived from 1729—1796. She ruled approximately from 1767 to 1796. During her rule she attempted to modernize Russia. Empress Catherine looked to the West to attract people to come and develop the vast territories that she had conquered. The czarina invited the Mennonites to come and occupy her land and to raise the agricultural standards in Russia. They were given a number of promises and privileges such as no military service, free homesteads, tax-exemption for several years, and self government in local affairs. She offered some financial assistance for three to five years to help them get started. This seemed quite attractive to many. They settled in the Ukraine and later spread to various parts of the country. That is how the Mennonite people came to be in Russia with their origins being Swiss, Dutch, German, and Polish. Catherine opened the doors of Russia for religious freedom to the many Christians who were being persecuted throughout the then known European Continent for their faith.

New Settlements Established

T he first group settled near Alexanderwohl, now Zaparosche. Later, groups settled about 75 miles north, along the Molotoschna River in the Taurida Region. This is where our ancestors settled. They started as pioneers, but once settled, they soon prospered. Their settlement comprised several counties and they had their own local economy under the State. As I mentioned previously, they had a common language and common religious faith. All spoke a "Low German." There is no official script of this language, though in recent years some have put it into writing. In school they were taught the script language of German, and in their homes they spoke Low German. This has persisted to the present generation.

Our family was part of this movement. My grandparents were born in Alexanderwohl. When I revisited Russia in 1978, I had the privilege of visiting this small village where my grandparents had grownup. As a people, they became prosperous in the Ukraine. They were good farmers, hard working, and thrifty. They started coming to the Ukraine towards the third quarter of the eighteenth century. But near the end of the nineteenth century it got too crowded, so the people moved on to other parts of Russia.

The larger area of Siberia, where our people settled, was not totally unpopulated, there were small as well as large villages surrounding the area. Those people were mostly descendants of former political criminals who were sent to Siberia by the czarist government for political and other crimes. These people differed from the common peasant population of other parts of Russia. They were very hospitable, clean, respectful, and trustworthy in their dealings, as Gerhard Fast in his book, *In Den Steppen Sivernes* (pg. 35), well described these people and their life styles in this region.

Family History

Right after the turn of the century, from 1908 to 1911, new lands were opened in Siberia. Several thousand people moved from the Ukraine to central Siberia. Since homesteads were being opened-up in that region, they took advantage of the opportunity and moved to central Siberia.

Mennonites settled a large section, comprised of thirty-seven villages covering two counties. That is where our family settled.

My grandfather, Nicholai Block, was a schoolteacher. As his family grew, he looked for land for farming because teaching was not a very lucrative vocation. My grandmother was Katharina Janzen Block. The Janzens were short and stout, but the Blocks were tall people. There were nine brothers, and all were tall men. Before their move to Siberia, our grandparents lived in the Samara region where grandfather taught school. That also was the region where my mother was born. But when land opened up, they joined the movement and arrived in Siberia in the spring of 1908.

My dad's parents arrived in this area in 1909. They came with absolutely nothing except the clothes on their backs. My paternal grandfather died from small pox shortly after they arrived in Siberia. My dad was nine years old. It has been told that his grandparents fled from Poland with only a baby carriage and all that it could hold of their personal possessions. They had been prosperous people in Poland. My dad's mother had a sister who was married to a Mr. Bolt who had a younger brother who was still single. Because of the circumstances they found themselves in, it was decided that my grandmother should marry this man because she would need a man around to help run the farm and do the heavy agricultural work. That man was not very energetic or industrious. He was a gambler and spent his life gambling away the family resources. He sold the Rogalsky's beautiful stock of horses for inferior Russian horses so that he would have some money. My father could never come up to his expectations and was abused and mistreated by him continually. As a young child my dad had to work very hard in the fields and where ever work was available. When we were ready to leave Russia, Dad's stepfather said, "You mean to tell me that you are leaving all of this behind and go to some far off place that you know nothing about? Not me, I'll wait until you are settled and then I will give it some thought." Of course, they were not able to follow and he was subsequently banished soon after we left. He became ill during the banishment and was sent home. He died shortly after that.

My dad had two sisters, Katharina and Elizabeth, also one brother, Frank. Katharina married a Mr. Tows and had five children, Johann, Abram, Katya, Elizabeth, and Frieda. Dad's mom was a very efficient woman. After we arrived in the United States, Dad's sisters and brothers were placed in forced labor camps, and Dad's mother had to take care of the grandchildren. She finally wrote to us in California and told us of her sad situation. She had no money for food and clothes and she had only one old military uniform to wear. We gathered some good clothes, new and used, and sent her a package. The package was many months in route, and we thought that she had received it. The package was returned to us and it was threadbare and tattered, but everything was still in it. Then she wrote us a letter and told us they had shown her the package, but the duty on it was so expensive she had no way of paying it so the package was returned to us. I remember that so well. I grieved for days over the injustice and tyranny of the situation. That incident occurred in the years 1938–1939. The letters were written on any kind of scrap paper because paper was so scarce, but our postal service always saw to it that we received those letters.

My dad was a man of few words. He worked hard and spoke very little. When we used to visit at the grandparents' house I would sit and listen to him talk with the other men, but at home he was too tired to talk much after a hard days work. My mother told me that he had a deep spiritual experience when he was eighteen years of age but really never talked about it. When he would be out in the vineyard pruning, he would sing to himself and the outdoors *"My God and I go in the Fields Together."* My dad enjoyed playing the Balalaika in the evenings.

The climate also should be mentioned. Central Siberia is deeply inland, not close to any ocean that would moderate temperatures. Because of this the weather is hot in the summertime and extremely cold in the winter season. The summers are dry, though crop failures were rare. Summers also are short. Seeding time is from mid-April to the beginning of May. Wheat always is planted first, then barley, and then oats. This may be because wheat is the main cash crop and barley and oats were mostly raised for feed for the stock. The days are long in summer. The sun rises about 5:00 A.M. and sets just before 10:00 P.M. Because of that, crop growth is rapid. Grain, which is seeded by end of April, is ready for harvest by late August or early September. The first snow usually comes around the beginning of October. The land is very fertile so that even in dry years crops usually produced twenty-five to thirty bushels per acre. They also raised potatoes and other vegetables for their own food supply that included sunflowers for the seeds and oil. The men really enjoyed eating roasted sunflower seeds while socializing in the evenings.

Mother related, "When the harvest time came, I had to ride the horse to pull a device used for threshing grain. After a while, we hooked up a circle of eight horses to go round and round to drive the threshing machine, and then I had to drive the horses to make them go around. I really had the job of a cowboy. I preferred that to housework.

"In October, we had to bring the animals in and hand feed them, since there was no grazing available to them. In April, the spring thaw began. Seeding was begun in May. In August, harvesting began. We had five months of spring and summer, then seven months of winter. We harvested carrots and potatoes approximately at the same time and stored them in the cellar and covered them with sand and they kept very well until the next harvest. We did no canning of food and, of course, there was no other way of preservation. We raised onions and garlic and round watermelons and we put them onto wooden trays. The cabbage we made into sauerkraut and sometimes we put cucumbers into the sauerkraut. We used a lot of cabbage. The cabbage was very juicy. We raised all the food we ate.

"There was a great famine in parts of Russia 1921. They ate corn in place of bread in some of the areas. In Siberia we did not have that famine. We always had bread. We also raised our own tomatoes. Dad did not like tomatoes, but he learned to eat them in the US. We used the tomatoes in our cooking. We would cover them with straw for the winter and they would keep very well."

My mother is Anna Block Rogalsky and was born in the Ukraine as was as my grandmother, Katharina Janzen Block. My grandfather, Nicholai Block, also came from the Ukraine. Their parents had immigrated from Holland. Our ancestry on my mother's side is Holland Dutch. My father was Heinrich David Rogalsky, born in south Russia. His father was born in Poland and his name was David Rogalsky, and his mother's maiden name was Helena Ewert. My dad's grandmother's maiden name was Friesen and his grandfather's name was Frank Rogalsky. Jacob Reimer who is a relative of my dad's family told that to me. He informed me that the grandparents had a beautiful home and that Grandfather was a remarkable tailor.

My dad had a favorite uncle, Jacob Rogalsky, who immigrated with his wife Sara to South America soon after we came to the United States. Many years later they immigrated to Canada, and we had the privilege of meeting them.

My mother relates the story, "We moved to Siberia, I was not quite five years old. We started our move in March and didn't arrive until late in August. I can only remember small bits and pieces. I know how we arrived. We stayed in a neighboring village and spent the night. My father was a land agent and he had been there previously with some other men and had measured off a section of land and laid claim to it so we knew where we would be. I don't know if we took the entire trip with horses and sleighs or if we took the train part of the way. We arrived in the wilderness, the men dug down several feet into the ground and made what is known as a sod house. We lived in the sod house until we could build our house."

When my mother arrived in Siberia with her parents they spent the first few nights with people in a neighboring section who were Lutherans. The Lutherans did not know how to cultivate the soil so they worked for and with the Mennonites, who were able to teach them.

Mother continued, "The first year we couldn't plant anything. We had to prepare the soil first. So we had no crop the first year. We had to haul the wood for our home from long distances. My father was very sick. I don't know what kind of sickness he had, but he was very sick. Therefore, my eldest brother, Jacob, had to go for the wood. He joined the wood hauling party of men. He was just a young man. It took many weeks to haul that wood and on his return home one of his horses died. That I can recall very well how hard my brother wept because the horse died and the other men divided the load up with their loads so he could take a lighter load with his one horse until he finally reached home.

"Of course, then we had to buy another horse. You had to have two horses. We had hardships one after another and could not finish the house that year. The outside was finished but the inside was not insulated with wallboard, so the house was so cold in the winter that the water in the bucket by the stove froze over. The next year we were able to finish the house and we were able to sow a crop of grain, so the subsequent year was better.

"For heating, we only had tumbleweeds, and that heat was very quick hot and very quick cold. No lasting heat. We raked up tumbleweeds and used it for fuel such as it was. The landscape was flat. I had never seen mountains until we reached China.

"The Russians did not know how to cultivate the plains. That is why they wanted the Mennonites there to cultivate the land. That is why they offered such fabulous home-steading opportunities. So after we had grain, we had straw. We had animals, cows and horses, and we used the ma-nure. It was dried and used as fuel. This gave good steady warming heat. That's how I grew up.

"We still had no schools. My father was a teacher and he did not want to teach again because he could not sup-port his family. They did not pay the schoolmasters very well. He taught us in our home. He farmed and also was the village schoolmaster.

"Each village had their own private school. In 1908, a school was built in our village and my father taught. The girls went to school five years and the boys went seven years. They had to learn to read and write and, of course, they learned mathematics. The families that had money could send their children away to school for more education, however most only received seven years of school. My brother Peter, the one who remained in Russia, also received extra years of schooling, as did Henry Isaak. They went on to government sponsored schools (That is what Henry Isaak talks about in his book, Our Life Story and Escape).

"We moved onto land that had never been cultivated. There were only two other families in the village of

Blumenort when our family arrived. The village eventually grew to about thirty families. Because my father was ill during a part of the first summer, our house did not get finished before winter set in. The family moved into a mere shell of a house. Winters in Siberia are severe and long. Temperatures often drop to minus 30 or 40 degrees centigrade. The heating materials were tumbleweeds, wood from the creek, or whatever could be reclaimed from nature.

"In the spring, diphtheria struck the village. There was no medical help available other than a pharmacist and simple medications. They could not stop the disease, and in our

Anna Block (my mother) and Peter Block (my uncle) who was banished and later killed soon after we left Russia.

family four children died. They were not little children. The oldest sister, Katherine, was twenty-one, a brother, Jacob, was eighteen and a sister, Mary, was thirteen, another brother, David, was seven years of age. All four died within a two-week period.

"It was a very difficult time for my mother. My brother John was a baby, and Mother would take care of him, as well as my very sick siblings. Everybody thought the baby certainly would die because my mother took care of the sick children and then took care of the baby. By God's providence, the baby never got sick. He lived through it all. A few years later my youngest brother, Jacob, was born." (A note of explanation: I am told that when a family member died, and other children were born after that death, often the newborn was given name of the one who had died. Therefore, Mother had two brothers named Jacob.

My mother related the frustration and anxiety when her older brother Peter had to leave for war.

"This was in the fall of 1918. It was during the early days of the Revolution, after the czar had been overthrown and a temporary republic was set up. Of course, this republic was immediately attacked by the second revolutionary movement, the communists. My brother was to go on the side of the republic. They didn't have uniforms, so they simply wore their own clothes. She recalls, Grandmother fixing his backpack.

"Peter served in the medical corps. The men received a few weeks of training to take the wounded off the battlefield. He was a noncombatant, and the Russians honored that preference. Since my brother was sent to the front right away, my father wanted to go see him before he was sent away. Peter Isaak, who later became my stepfather was just returning from a trip where he had gone as a village representative.

When he met my father at the station, he said, 'Mr. Block, don't go, you will never make it.' Traveling in those days was too difficult. "My father was a man of determination, however, he arrived at the place where Peter was, one day late. The men had already been sent away.

"The Russian rail was infested with vermin, body lice, ticks, and fleas. It was very dangerous, and my father got some of the lice and was bitten. He developed spotted fever (bubonic plague). He was home just three days and he got the fever. No one survived this illness. He lost consciousness in three days, and we called Dr. Voth. He said there is no hope and he never returned to see him again.

"My mother and I took care of him. We were in total quarantine. We had to hang black flags outside our doors as warnings so no one would come near. The disease was very contagious. They said in a family the illness would go up age wise, but not down. As a result none of the rest of us in our family got sick. My older siblings were already dead and I was the oldest at home and I was fifteen years old.

"These were trying times for the entire country. Many people came from other places begging for food. Even some of the people in our village did not have enough to eat. However, we always had enough food.

"Clothing was very difficult to come by. Out of desperation, Mother would cut up canvas, which had been used on the self-binder for harvesting, to make clothes for the children.

"Mother was longing to hear from Peter. He had been sent off to the front, she knew, but there was never any word about him. I remember that one late winter evening, a neighbor lady, in whose house the village office was located, came to our door. She knocked and called out for us to open the door for her, that she had news. She said she had a letter. Mother opened it up, and there was a message that Peter was alive, that he had been wounded and taken prisoner by the "Red" (Communists). Peter had been a prisoner and placed in a hospital. His injury, a leg wound, was not too serious. After a time of furlough, he stayed with relatives in that region, since home was just too far away to come home.

My mother recalls that the afternoon that her father died, her mother told her to call uncle Henry and her uncle Frank Janzen. Immediately, the family cleared out the house and disinfected it. "We did not have the disinfectants like we have today. We burned sulfur in the room to disinfect it. My mother took my father's clothing and heated them in the large bake-oven that was built into our house. Then Father's bedding was placed in large sacks, buried in the ground and left for a time.

"The funeral was held in a larger house across the street from ours. It was a stormy day in February 1919. Snow was blowing. Only adults were allowed to go to the cemetery because of the terrible weather outside that day. Grandma had a hard time alone. She was left with five children. They were Anna, fifteen, Henry, fourteen, Frank, seven; John five; Jacob was three years old."

My mother relates that Grandmother was not too well herself. My mother took on performing the household tasks. "Grandma was forced to depend on neighbors and friends. They took advantage of her, particularly in the matter of taking care of our farm machinery, which Grandfather always had cared for so meticulously. Sometimes it was returned in not as good condition as it had been. Grandmother's difficulty was increased by this carelessness and by the awareness of Granddad's meticulous care for his equipment.

"My mother's younger brother took over the farm, and he was very poor. He had no farm equipment, but we had the farm equipment such as a threshing machine, and it was stipulated that he had to harvest our crops first and then he could harvest his. He would get ours all harvested, and then winter would be upon us. Then he could not harvest his grain. So it had to be stacked on the plains and left out in the field all winter until spring. This meant he had to live off of our crop. Therefore, we could not sell any wheat. We couldn't let him go hungry. He promised that he would return his share the next fall when he would harvest his crops. So that fall when we went to harvest the crops the communists came and took it all away. So we lost everything, and so did he. They had five little boys.

4
Communities

My mother continues her story, "Winters were long and cold with short days. Sunrise came at approximately 8:00 A.M. and sunset about 4:00 P.M.. Temperatures often dropped as low as minus 30 or 40 degrees centigrade. Severe storms prevailed. This is one of the reasons for living in villages instead of on individual farms. If residences had been separated by miles, communal life and a school system would have been impossible and exceedingly dangerous. The people lived on plots of about five to seven acres. Every place in the village was the same size, because the entire settlement was planned and laid out according to the plan. Each village had a certain amount of land that was divided into a given number of residences with yards.

"Blumenort, where my grandparents settled, had twenty-three families and Petrovoka, where we lived later, had thirty.

The surrounding farmland also was divided into strips of a given width and length. Each owner had the same size field, because all homesteads were the same size. On one side of the village was an area of communal pastureland, which was not subdivided. On this pasture, all the livestock were pastured from early spring, about mid-April, until the snow fell. Herdsmen were hired, contracted to a family who hired whatever help they needed. Usually these were native Siberians or of some other ethnic group. Living quarters were provided for them. The residents turned their cows out on the street in the morning, and a herdsman would start at one end of the one-street village and drive the cattle to the pasture. The herd increased as he moved along. They stayed out all day.

"The herd of cows was followed by a herd of calves and sheep. After seeding time, a herd of horses were kept in a separate field. In the evening the calves and sheep came home first and then the cows. As the herdsman drove the respective herds along the street, someone from each family was there to meet their own stock and see to it that they turned in at their yard. The cows then were tied to a stake and milked by hand. They stayed there until the next day when they were turned out onto the street in the morning for pasturing. Horses were not returned home but housed in a common corral at the end of the village, close to the herdsman's house. If a farmer wanted to use one or more of his horses the next day, he went out in the evening or early in the morning to the corral and caught his horse. He then returned it to the herd in the field later in the day or to the corral in the evening.

"Water was available in water holes in the birch woods. The white birch forests are common in Siberia. The landscape is spotted with small woods, which grow around a

depression and in the spring is full of water from the melting snow. More snow is stored up among the trees and lasts
longer than in open fields, so that many of these depres-
sions provide water for stock all summer. By the way, they
served as swimming holes for boys and girls in the summer, though not all at the same time, because swimming
suits were not known.

"Once winter set in, all of our livestock was housed in a
barn attached to our living quarters. Although the barns
were not heated, being attached to the house made the barn
warmer and it was easier to care for the animals without
going outside.

"Each kind of stock was in its own section of the barn.
The horses, six or eight, were tied on two sides of a crib
with a rack mounted above the crib for feeding straw or
hay. The crib also served feed chaff mixed with small
amounts of grain mixed with water. The crib also was used
for watering the horses. The sections were partitioned off
by a wall about four-foot high. In their sections, the cows
stood in stanchions all in one row. They also were fed by a
long trough, but this was on the ground, whereas the horses
trough was about three feet from the ground. Although the
horses were tethered to the crib, they had some room to
move around but the cows stayed in their stanchions all
winter. They could stand up or lie down but could not leave
their place. They did well, they were well fed, calves were
born there and the cows were milked there. On warmer
days, a few times during the long winter, they were turned
loose outside. They walked around in the snow for awhile,
but usually turned into the barn on their own accord.

"The barn was cleaned twice a day all winter long. The
dung was piled up in the yard where the process of decom-
position went on, which prepared the materials later to be
turned into heating fuel.

"One of the major sources of heating fuel was animal waste. During the long winter, all of the barnyard manure was placed in a pile in the yard where it was allowed to decompose until spring. In the spring, after seeding time, this manure was processed. The processing consisted of thoroughly mixing it and placing it on the threshing floor, spread out. Horses were ridden around on it until it became a smooth paste. The top of the manure was leveled off and it was allowed to dry for about two weeks. Before it was thoroughly dry, it was cut into bricks, and the bricks were set on edge to complete the drying process. The dried bricks were then stacked in a shelter waiting the winter. This was our heating fuel.

"In the last years they had a machine that would process the raw manure and press the material out in square "logs." These then were cut into the desired lengths, about ten feet. As the decomposed manure came out neatly from the machine, a board-sled drawn by one horse, ridden by a boy, hauled the bricks to a drying place in the yard. After that, the drying process continued pretty much as the hand-made bricks.

"Lamps during the long winter evenings were home-made to burn animal fat, which had been processed as the animals were slaughtered for food. That is how people in the villages met their essential needs, which differed from those living in cities."

5
Prosperity

My mother relates that, "They started with nothing and yet they accomplished so much in spite of their adversity." In less than a decade before the Revolution they had developed a well-established farming operation." By the time the Revolution came, Mother remembers, "That we had sufficient means to meet all our needs. Seven or eight horses, which provided our needed power; about a dozen cows, sheep, hogs, and chickens supplied meat and other nutrients. We had also acquired some farm machinery, which most people in the village did not have. Our family had an American-made McCormick self-binder harvester that harvests the grain and ties it into bundles automatically. The bundles are carried along by machine on to a platform until about ten or twelve bundles are accumulated. Then they were loaded on wagons and hauled to the threshing machine, which operated by horsepower, but was the most advanced equipment available at that time. Most of the people threshed grain by placing it on a threshing floor, here they laid out grain several inches deep and rolled it with a threshing stone. This stone was limestone hewn out in a hexagon shape. It was drawn by two horses; the stone rolled over and over the layer of stalks of grain until all the grain was threshed out of the heads. The straw was then picked up off the grain with large wooden forks. The grain and chaff that remained were scooped up and separated by hand-operated, wind blowing machines. The chaff was blown out to the rear, and the grain was dropped out in front. Our threshing machine did this whole thing in one operation, much faster and more efficiently. Later on, further cleaning had to be done by another type of blowing machine."

About 6 My Father

My parents came to Siberia from South Russia in 1908. Dad's parents came in 1909 from south Russia to Siberia. He had one brother, Frank, and two sisters. One sister died from small pox at the same time his father died with small pox. The sister who lived was named Katharina, and they called her Tina. She is the mother of Katya Tessman, whom I met in June of 1996. We discovered each other from an ad in the Mennonite paper *Die Bote,* and they came to visit us in California.

Then, after his father died, he had four half-sisters with the Bolt name.

Dad was in the military for the Whites, also known as the Republic. He was in the "second row." He always had to follow close to the front to take care of the wounded. Also, he handled the munition wagons with the horses. My dad was taken captive by the Reds during the Revolution. The officer in charge of my dad threatened to kill him, so he made his escape. He fled by rail, holding on to the top of boxcars or under the cars, whichever way he could hide and travel. The Russians also had outside steam rooms, and often he would hide out in those.

He came home on Christmas Eve night and he was covered with vermin. He could not be allowed into the house. He had to remove his clothes before he could enter the house. His clothes were bundled up and burned. He was a young man and totally exhausted, at times he was not even coherent. He knew he was home and that was all.

When he had recuperated he was drafted again. This time he was able to stay close to home and work in the mill. He didn't get any salary, but this was his military service since he didn't take up arms. The military recognized noncombatant service. You may recall that was a part of the agreement the government made when they came to homestead land and developed it. They would not be required to take up arms during military conflict. This is part of Catherine the Great's Mandate. Dad was around eighteen years of age at that time. Not yet married to my mother.

The 7 Poor Economy

Mother continues. "In 1919, my brother Peter was drafted again, my younger brothers were too young, and I was the oldest one at home. Many of the young men were drafted for the purpose of receiving wheat at the granaries in the city. Peter had the good fortune to have had a good elementary education. He was assigned work as a grain receiver. The farmers were not allowed to keep any for themselves, they were paid for the grain with money. We paid thousands of rubles for just one loaf of bread. The money was worthless, but the grain still had to be delivered. Most of the farmers managed to keep some for their own food, although sometimes they were at great risk for doing so. While Peter was receiving grain, he occasionally had a chance to come home. The city was only about twenty-five miles away, so on weekends and certain other occasions he made it home.

"My mother became ill and she was in bed all summer long. She had serious trouble with her stomach and had to drink all kinds of potions that were brewed for her.

"We had enough food because we were on the farm, but clothing was very scarce. So sometimes Peter would manage to bring a new gunnysack or two home to make clothing for family members. We asked him how he got the gunnysacks. "Well," he said, "in counting sometimes there is a surplus" This all may sound quite trivial, but it was very important in our lives. My Uncle John relates how wonderful it was to receive a new shirt made from one of those gunnysacks."

The Wedding

After about three and half years, in the summer of 1922, Grandma was married to Mr. Peter Isaak. They moved to the village where Mr. Isaak had his home. This meant a new school for my mother's brothers. The schools were one large room where one teacher taught six grades. They sat at long tables with a bench attached, and there was a shelf under the table to place their materials. Paper was very scarce. They wrote mostly on slate boards. Chalk also was scarce and so chicken bones were burned to the right texture and they made good writing tools.

At that time, my mother's brother, Henry, had been sick with tuberculosis for several months. About eight days after the wedding, Henry died. My mother and the rest of the brothers, Frank, John, and Jacob moved to the new village named Petrovoka. Peter, however, had married his boyhood

sweetheart and they stayed in the family house, until they
bought their own.

Mother continues, "Some three years later, while we
were living in Petrovka, my brother Frank got seriously ill
and died. His death was very traumatic for John; they were
just two years apart in age and very close. He was thirteen
and John was eleven years old."

My mother married my dad, Henry Rogalsky, the first
winter after her mother was married to Peter Isaak. There
were a lot of social activities in the village and so they
started going out together. As my father came courting
my mother, the village young men observed him riding
into the village on a wonderful horse. They were wondering who this stranger was and they were prepared to
attack him, however my father was an accomplished horse-
man and was able to evade them. Later, when the young
men realized he was courting my mother, they allowed
him in. Mother had been the "queen" in the village and
the other young men also had hoped to have a chance to
court her, but that was not to be.

"The wedding was on November 2, 1924. It was a cold
day. It was a home wedding. In the summer time, we had
large outdoor weddings. The barns were used for the fes-
tivities; straw was put on the floor. In the winter, we had to
use the house. A sheep was butchered and soup was made
for lunch for the guests who arrived from other villages.
Then at 2:00 P.M., the wedding ceremony was begun. They
had Faspa; (a traditional Sunday supper) then they had a
program, singing, recitations, and sermonetts. We then had
supper, after which the bride took her veil off. It was re-
placed by a large bow as a head covering."

My mother never wore a prayer bonnet, nor did my
grandmother. So at mothers wedding, she used the bow as

her head covering. " The single women did not wear head coverings of any kind. Only married women wore head coverings."

"She was now the wife, and the bride was given a sweet sweiback, then they served cold ham and sweibacks and other cold foods for supper. At 9:00 P.M. the wedding was over for the older people, and the young peoples' time began. Dancing, music, playing games, until 2:00 A.M."

They had a good time. My mother really chuckled at this. I believe she actually relived the moment as we were talking. She danced at her own wedding. I know my dad loved to play the Balalaika, but in the United States, as far as I know, he never danced, although he did try to do the Kossack dance once when we first came to America.

My mother continued her story. "There was no honeymoon or getting away. The next day was a full working day. I had to help clean up from the wedding, kill geese, and dress them. We had to move to my husband's family house. There was no room at my mother's house because of the Isaak's living there. I had to wash the clothes and help pack food supplies for the winter. In those years, there was very little available to buy for wedding gifts. So we received very little. A few towels, etc. We had to buy all the dishes and utensils we needed for our own housekeeping. We lived in the Bolt household one-year, and then in autumn we were able to move out. We moved to Blumenort, and we were able to make an exchange with another couple so we were able to move closer to the Isaaks (my parents) and we were able to rent land. Our house was a small village-house with hard dirt floors in Petrovaka. One neighbor lived between our houses, they were the George Klippensteins. We shared land and equipment. We didn't have any threshing machines. The Isaaks had all of that. So, they shared in the harvesting. Dad worked for them when they harvested, and they allowed him use of the machinery."

I was born on August 20, 1925. I was born prematurely and delivered by a midwife. My grandmother was present at my birth. My Uncle Jacob recently told me it was a very sad situation. I was so small. I weighed only three-and-a-half pounds. No one thought that I would live. If I had been born in the winter months, I probably would not have survived.

The first month I was fed with an eyedropper. I was kept warm with bottles filled with hot water. My dad made a little wooden box to put me in and later Dad made a cradle for me. Mother continues, "After that first month you were stronger and you were able to nurse. I did not have enough milk to nurse you, but I gave you fresh cows milk and you grew and after a few months you started to eat cereal with milk, and bread soaked in milk."

When I was first born, I was jaundiced, and it appeared I would not live. The women all encouraged my mother to allow me to die because I would be mentally deficient since I was only an eight-month baby. I learned to walk before I was a year old.

A year later on October 1, 1926, my sister Helen was born. After Helen was born, I had the measles and I was very sick. Helen had a malady called an English sickness. She always sat with her legs crossed and she did not walk until she was two years old. Helen's legs continued to bother her for years.

Anna was born November 29, 1927. Anna learned to walk at fourteen months. My grandmother would tell me that she could hear me coming down the village road to their house. They tell me I was a chatter-mouth and talked continually.

Dreaming of
a Different Future

Mother relates, "As long as I can remember, I heard people talking about going to America even when we lived in the village of Blumenort, where we lived before her mother married Peter Isaak. I heard people telling stories that we were going to be able to go to America. When people spoke of America, they generally meant North America. There was a big migration of Mennonites to Mexico in 1925."

Mother continues, "There was a Dr. Neufelt who came from Canada about this time to examine the health of our people. One important aspect of health requirements was the condition of our eyes. There was much trachoma, an infection of the eyes with which most everyone was afflicted, at least a touch of it. It was known that people with this disease would not be admitted to Canada or the United

States. This is why Dr. Neufelt came to treat people so they would qualify to be admitted. Mother had a very severe case of trachoma. Dr. Neufelt operated on her. The soviet authorities were not at all sympathetic to Dr. Neufelt's endeavors and gave him an order to leave within twenty-four hours. This happened right after my mother's operation. Thanks to the good care of some of the nurses, she came through it all right.

"In those days, another wheat delivery was ordered. All grain had to be delivered to the government granaries. I remember a specific incident during threshing time. The little boys were told to stay in the house for a length of time. They were not to know what was happening. It turned out that my grandfather, Mr. Isaak, and some other men had secretly dug a big pit and were filling it with wheat. Then they stacked the barn full of straw and chaff for feed for the stock to eat during the winter. It had to be hidden this way for protection against authorities that might come and search for hidden grain. This plan of burying the wheat would make it very difficult for the inspectors to find anything. Some people just poured wheat into their piles of chaff, but sometimes they were caught when inspectors poked around in the chaff. When they poked deeply enough, they found the grain. It wasn't expected that the wheat would be delivered to the government free. They were being paid for it, but the money was worthless. Therefore, people tried to hide whatever they could. It was a matter of survival.

"A creamery was opened in our village. Butter was shipped in small barrels, and my dad was a gifted craftsman in making wooden articles. Therefore, he was challenged to learn the trade of making barrels. He accepted, and became the official cooper for the creamery."

"Since storing butter and other dairy products requires refrigeration, an ice cellar was built. It was dug into the ground with a sod roof covering it so that the heat would not penetrate it. During the winter blocks of ice up to five feet thick were broken loose from the nearby man-made lake along the local creek. The lake was made by damming up the creek with an earthen dam. The ice was hauled on sleds to the cellar where a crew of men with sledgehammers broke the ice up into blocks. When the cellar was full, the ice was covered with clean straw to retard melting. This ice in the cellar lasted all summer and was used as needed for cooling. The next winter the process was repeated and the cellar was again filled up with ice."

10 Capitalistic Taxation

My mother continues, "There also was a special taxation, a capitalist tax. People who were a little better off than others were called Kulak and they had to pay this special tax." I know Grandfather Isaak was required to pay it, and of course, he did. "Our neighbor, Henry Janzen, a minister, also had to pay this tax. He did not have enough to pay it on his own, so the officials told him to go and see his "brothers" in the congregation to help him. He never asked them to pay, but only let them know his financial need and the congregation met his need, and he was kept out of prison."

My grandfather Isaak was listed as a Kulak. Since there was more work than he could handle, a young man, Henry Schmidt, was hired to help for several years. Also, a young lady was hired to help and to stay with us. Her name was

Anna Friesen. They were happy to work for us. These people had not reported any irregularities nor where they unhappy with their jobs, but the principle of the matter was that if you hired someone to work for you, you must be benefiting from someone else's efforts and this was not allowed by soviet rules.

Dad also was listed among the Kulaks because we also had a young boy and a young girl Margaret Friesen in our home to help with the work.

Secret Preparations to Leave Russia

At about 1927 or 1928, a new settlement was made in eastern Siberia, in the Amur River region. John Isaak, my step-uncle, and his family moved to that region and took up new land for homesteading. They were only a few miles from the Amur River, which forms the border between Russia and China. During the winter of 1928, he returned to central Siberia where he had his permanent home and served as a settlement representative, specifically, to buy cattle. He bought a lot of cattle, but while he was there, he also communicated some information to our family. He told them he had been to China several times. There was an opportunity to cross the border into China, and from there we might have a chance to go to America.

Mr. Henry Isaak told my dad about the possibility of being able to get out of Russia. He and my mother talked about this for several days. He would be the only one from his family that would be able to leave. My mother was at near term with her fourth pregnancy and it would be very risky. They made the decision to go and began to make preparations to that end.

The children were not told any of this, but the adults in the family began to make arrangements to that end. The farms and the cattle were going to be sold and they would try to migrate to the Amur region. The planning was done in secret, and, in due time, the older children were told what was happening and sworn to secrecy. If the information leaked out, it could mean the deaths of the parents, life imprisonment, or execution. The children would then be sent to a soviet orphan home. The children were told that we would be going to the Amur region to live. Preparations proceeded quietly.

Margaret Friesen and her sister, Anna, who was older, were orphaned and Anna begged my parents to take Margaret with them. So my father arranged for the proper paper work to be made out so that it would be legal to take Margaret with them to another country as their own child. It was signed and noted by the proper authorities, so Margaret Friesen took the name of Rogalsky until she arrived in America. Her sister Anna was engaged to be married, so she chose to stay behind.

After we were in Reedley a few years, the Nickels from Shafter, who had no children, wanted her to come into their family. After a lengthy discussion, it was determined that perhaps the Nickels were related to the Rogalsky family. Margaret was given the option to go and live with the Nickels in Shafter. They promised her an education and a better life than we could give her. The Nickels then asked, "How can we help you?" Dad asked the Nickels to pay

Margaret's passage fare if at all possible. They were happy to do that. Margaret then went to beauty school and became a successful hairdresser.

She later married Henry Regehr who was one of the bachelors who helped my parents carry us onto the train in Russia. They made their home in Morrow Bay, California.

While we were in China life was so very difficult for my dad, so Margaret needed to do house work for a German family of means, who were living in Harbin. My dad would visit her every Sunday to make sure that she was alright. She enjoyed her work and they took very good care of her.

I met her sister, Anna Harms, Anna's son and daughter-in-law in Russia in 1978. That was a very special experience for me. I learned at that time that she and her husband had been sent on to slave labor camps and her husband died there. She was so thankful that we had taken her sister with us to freedom and safety.

The Crossing

Our family that came to America was a union of two families, the Isaaks and the Blocks. You remember that my step-grandfather's name was Peter P. Isaak and that he had children of his own when he married my grandmother. The ones who came were Grandfather Isaak and Grandmother Block Isaak, Uncle John and Marie Isaak, who developed the plan to leave Russia and who led the way. Also coming were their son John and daughter Olga (Brandt), Uncle Peter D. and Helena Isaak and their children, Anna Janzen, Helen, Betty Carson, Peter, George, and John (born in China). Uncle Henry P. and Anna Isaak and their children Henry, Peter, and Anna, (born in China) all live in and around Dinuba. Uncle Abram and Margaret Klassen, (Margaret was the sister to John, Peter and Henry Isaak,) children, Abe and Peter. Mr. Henry and Anna Rogalsky (my parents) and children: Katharine Sylvester, Helen Pauls, Anna Simon, Mary Nickel (born in China), Uncle John Block, and Jacob Block. David Janzen, Henry Regehr, and Margaret Friesen were the "singles" that also were in our group.

Among those who remained behind were Uncle Peter Block, and his family, who decided to wait because of his wife's family. Her parents were aged and ailing. Peter and his wife felt they could not leave them behind. His last comment to his mother, who is also my grandmother, was, "Don't worry about us, we'll make it, somehow. I can get along better without you than Agnes can get along without her parents." They never made it. Peter was banished soon after we left. They had made a brave attempt to come while we were still in China and staged a peaceful sit-in demanding to be allowed to leave Russia, but were not successful in that venture. After that, we received a few letters from him. One said he was no longer farming, but had become a laborer. The government had confiscated everything they had.

My mother continues her story. "As we were buying our ticket to go to Slavgorod, we observed a number of other people. We asked them, 'What are you doing here?' They said, "The same thing you are doing. We also want to go." Slavgorod was the first station. We all had to travel that way: The Pete Klippensteins, Henry Hieberts, Frank Loewens, and Jake Janzens. The Frank Loewens had only one tiny baby. The others all had grown children. They had gotten their tickets before us and they had already loaded all of their things into a railcar. Then Henry Hiebert, he was a big man, stood by the railcar door and said, 'All is full, there is no room for you.' We replied, 'We have our tickets, if we can't get on, we will be left behind.' I had packed all of the clothes we would need and I had prepared new baby clothes for my new baby, and we had our bedding with us. As it turned out, we, along with the Peter Isaaks and the Henry Isaaks, were forced to leave all of our baggage and possessions at the railroad station. All we could take with us was the food I had prepared. I had baked a couple of hams and toasted sweibacks.

"After the train got started and things were repacked, there was plenty of room. We could easily have taken along what we had prepared to take. So, it was with those other people. They had all the grown children and they pushed their way to the front and always were first."

When we boarded the train in the city of Slavgorad, Siberia, our destination was the Amur River Region. It was February 21, 1929. Three days later we arrived in Blagoveshchensk, the Capitol City of the Amur River basin on the eastern side of Siberia.

My step-uncle John Isaak by this time was under suspicion. He didn't come to the city to meet us. He wasn't allowed to travel more than two hours from home. He sent a neighbor to greet us in Blagoveshchensk.

Other people had joined us in our plan to escape. We were eleven families by this time, a total of sixty-two persons. Each family bought a horse and sleigh, which would be used in crossing the Amur River. As we traveled between the city and the designated place for our crossing of the River Amur, the snow was beginning to melt and it became soft and slushy making it very difficult to travel. It would have been easier to go by wagon, and certainly more comfortable, but we used sleighs because we needed them to cross the river. Since sleighs and wagons were commonly used by travelers, we did not arouse more suspicion by using sleighs.

We packed up and we started traveling. The men who had been hired to lead us were ready. We had full loads, so the men had to walk all the time. The horses couldn't walk very fast either. It was so cold, we were packed in tightly to keep warm. At night, we would stay in homes at the Russian villages. For night, we would scatter to different homes. The people were very friendly. They would cook us a hot meal. We had ridden all day on the sled with nothing to eat and we were cold. We would tell them we were going to a new settlement because we thought we would have more freedom there because the communist government would leave us alone. In the morning, we would gather again outside the village and continue with our slow travel.

On the last day before we were to cross over the border, the guide discovered that the village was full of Red Guard soldiers, so we couldn't cross there. We had to travel around the village to find a safer spot. It seemed as if we were just wandering, and the horses kept stumbling on the ice.

The trip was slow, and took longer than we had expected. It took three days. Mother relates that in one of the villages, suddenly, John Isaak was there. We must have been close to his village. He came in and met with the men in a room, secretly. There they agreed that since John was the one who had worked the whole plan out (even though he couldn't be with us) and since he had been in charge, in spite of his absence, every family would pay him a certain amount of money. We realized he wouldn't be able to sell any of his property without arousing suspicion. He was simply going to leave in the night, cross the border, and leave everything behind. The agreement was only verbal, but strong pledges were made, and John returned to his home. He sent a trusted friend, Thomas Friesen, who was to lead us across into China.

My mother was at term, in her fourth pregnancy. She had delivered her three other babies before her due date. Now, she was at term with her fourth pregnancy. We were placed at the end of the caravan just in case she would go into labor and cause the rest of the caravan to be in danger of discovery and be arrested or shot in the process of escape.

Mother continues her story. "We arrived at the designated place for our crossing. We were supposed to cross it about sundown, but the going was difficult and slow, and we finally arrived at midnight. Our leader, Thomas Friesen, had planned to just skirt around the village and go straight through to the river. However, in the darkness our guide got us lost, and we ended up going right through the middle of the village.

"There was a garrison of soldiers quartered in the village. We drove right past the military gate. Everything was quiet, the children didn't cry, and the dogs didn't bark. The guard of the village saw us go by but didn't get suspicious, because to them we were just another band of settlers coming into the area.

"Outside the village, a mile or two, the road dipped down to the river's edge. The river was frozen over, and the ice was covered with a layer of snow. This made for easy riding with sleighs, and a winter road had developed by common use. Our guide led us a little way along the river's edge and told us to stop. He and two other men rode for about half mile ahead. They found everything quiet. The sky was clear and the moon shone brightly. It was a beautiful night, near midnight.

"Our guide said in a solemn voice, 'The air is clear turn to the right.' Everyone turned his horse to the right and headed toward China. There was a bit of suspense in crossing the river though. The ice had frozen in big chunks, so it was very bumpy. One of the horses stumbled and fell. Fortunately, there were enough men to grab him by the harness and to help him back up to his feet, and away we went.

Tension was high for a few moments, but after a short time, when we didn't hear any shots fired, everyone calmed down and finished the trip across. Our guide led us directly to a store on the other side where we were expected.

"The people in China were friendly and hospitable. Arrangements had been made for us to spend the night in a store. In the morning it was noted there were no people living nearby, just two or three stores. Later on we discovered that these border stores existed for the most part for doing business in contraband merchandise. Some of the Russian people would sneak across the border to buy merchandise to take back into Russia either to use or to sell at a profit.

"Early the next morning there was no time to loiter around. Even the watering of the horses took too long. The men had seen a Russian mounted guard riding along the Russian side of the river counting the tracks of our sleighs. In all, eleven sleighs had escaped them. The presence of the mounted guard raised fears that the soldiers might possibly come across to take us back. The fact was, the rest of the world would never have known about it, or even cared. There was no one to stop the Russian authorities from having us brought back, but they did not pursue us." In all of these instances, I believe the profound grace of God in His protection was evident in our lives.

Seeking Refuge Inland

M other continues the story. "We simply harnessed up and drove all day to get to the next village. Our guide knew where the next village was, so we drove along the road, hoping at least to get away from the border we had crossed so recently. To our disappointment, the Amur River meandered considerably so that during the day we would find ourselves alongside of that river again and again as we proceeded toward the village we sought. Just before sundown, we approached the village. There were soldiers (Chinese) on the village streets. A small garrison was stationed there. As they saw us approaching, they dashed to their barracks and to their rifles and came out to meet us. They paired up, two soldiers per sleigh, one on each side. All they asked was, 'Do you have rifles?' in Russian. That seemed to be the only word in the Russian language they knew. Fortunately, we had no weapons of any kind.

"Later, the commander told us that when he saw women and children on all of the sleighs, he was fairly confident that we were not a camouflaged attack force, but some ordinary people fleeing to safety. He allowed us to stay in town only one night, because he did not want any trouble from the other side of the border. We spent the night there and met a Turkish man who spoke both Russian and Chinese. Our men engaged him as our interpreter and guide, and the next morning we started for another village away from the river, farther away from the border.

"About two miles before we reached the villages, early in the afternoon, we stopped at a farmhouse, where we were allowed to camp in the yard. Our women were suffering from the cold, so they were allowed to come in the house and warm up. Since my grandfather was an older man, he was allowed inside with my grandmother. A couple of our men went on into the village of Tchekade, just ahead of us, to talk to the captain of the garrison about allowing us to come there. When they explained to him that we were refugees, entire families, he allowed us to come.

"We arrived in the village and were directed to an oriental inn where we could stay. We were informed that we could not travel any further in their country without passports, so we stayed at this inn for some time. I remember that we had three rooms for sixty-two people. With such crowded conditions, we slept double-decked or triple-decked. The problem of passports became serious. Since we had none and couldn't travel without them, how were we to get them? Passports could only be obtained in the larger cities.

Fish
and Chips

My mother continues her story. "I have never eaten so much fish in all my life. The Chinese people brought us big fish. We all cooked on the same stove. We took turns. We bought the fish for several pennies. Our food was potatoes and fish. Potatoes we bought in the store.

"Then the men started to work out the details for our further travel. The mayor of the town came out to see us and asked us all kinds of questions. We were asked how much money we had. So we had to declare all that we had. We had in mind to immigrate to Canada. We would apply to Canada, then go to Canada, and we would all have our own money. Of course, we wanted to be self-sufficient. That was our plan but not God's plan. Then they said, 'We keep you here. You cannot travel anymore. You have to have Chinese visas, and we see to it that you get them. So you have to stay here and feed your horses. When you get ready to go we will buy your horses. However, until then you have to feed them and you have to buy the food.'

"We didn't hear anything about John Isaak. He couldn't come with us. He had really had an experience. He could not make any preparations. He and his wife were under constant surveillance. They acted just like nothing was happening and like they were planning on staying in Russia. At night, they started packing some clothes and food.

"They had a young couple who were newlyweds, whom they had taken in for the winter. One evening John Isaak was going to prayer meeting at the church. The young couple went to church with them. At the church John Isaak talked with the young couple and told them if you will keep quiet and not talk to anyone for three days about our activities, after we leave, you can have all of the property and equipment. The farm animals, cows, and horses, and everything.

"He had a shed, and in the privacy of that shed he had packed the sleigh he would take with him. He tucked his two children and wife into the sleigh and went out of the shed through the back door that night at 11:00 P.M. He had a horse harnessed to the sled and he took off so fast so that no one would catch him, however his wife fell out of the sleigh in the back and he didn't notice. Olga was crying, 'Daddy, Daddy, Mamma,' and he said to be quiet. 'We must not make any noise. We have to go.' She said, 'Mommy isn't here,' and he looked back and he saw her way back in the snow with her heavy snow pack on and he had to turn back to get her quickly. He packed her back into the sleigh, and they dashed across the border and joined us.

"John Isaak had a Chinese passport and he knew where to find us. We had decided to help them because he had to leave everything behind. He had not been able to sell any-thing, so he had no money.

"In the meantime, the Russians had gotten in touch with Chinese officers. They knew that somewhere in that village was a group from Russia that had crossed the border. But they couldn't go over by force and take them, because that would mean war with the Chinese. So, they thought they could bribe them by offering $1,000.00 per person when they would deliver us. The Chinese officers came and talked to our men. Our men said they would not go back under any circumstances. Then the Russians sent the Chinese again and begged us to talk with the Russians. The men refused to talk with the Russians. We remained in China.

Passports and Rough Roads

There was a bus line consisting of one or two busses between the village of Tchekade where we were staying and the city of Tzitsehar. It ran about every two days. It is interesting to note that these buses were American-made. Some were Model T Fords and one Model A, 1928 vintage.

"Upon return from the city, Uncle John Isaak came back to us with a photographer. They took pictures of us, and he took them back to the city and obtained passports for all of us. It was a bit expensive, but they were professional photographers whose main business was the providing of passports for refugees. After John obtained the passports, he sent them to us by bus. However, the commander said, 'These cannot be authentic passports since you haven't been anywhere outside our village'. He said, 'They must be counterfeit,' and so he confiscated them. Our men managed to persuade him to send a telegram to the city inquiring about them. There are all kinds of ways to execute a bribe, which they did, to get him to do it, and he received the answer back that the passports were genuine. Also, he was ordered to release them to us immediately. He seemed embarrassed about the bribe he had accepted and did not see us again.

"His officers for the army bought all of our horses. Because our horses were a larger breed than their small Mongolian horses, the Chinese paid more for them than we had paid originally in Russia. After being in the village for two more weeks, we chartered four buses (two Model T's, one Model A, and a Dodge truck with a canopy) to take us to our destination, the city of Tzitzehar. From there, after a night riding the train, we arrived at Harbin where we were going to be staying until we would be able to come to America."

My Uncle John relates, "That at the start of this leg of the trip, there was much excitement, especially among the young people and children. They had never ridden on a bus before. However the excitement wore off in a short while because of the huge bumps that tossed us up and down and frequently banged our heads on the roof of the bus. We were traveling about fifteen persons per bus. There weren't any roads, just trails. The bus driver wound through the mountains, which, in reality, were only rolling hills. These trails led across streams, creeks, and wider rivers. We had just crossed the Amur River on March 7, so this part of our trek was toward the end of March. It happened that this was the very last trip the busses would be taking until the water froze over again the next winter. The waters were already beginning to thaw. During the summer months, travelers relied on boats for transportation.

"Thawing made gaping holes in the narrow trails, full of sticky mud. Sometimes the passengers were needed to help push the wheels up out of the holes. At other places, the ice had started to melt on top, even though it was still firm underneath. On occasion a driver unloaded half his load, drove across, and unloaded. He then came back and reloaded and went back across. The last time through, one wheel started to crack through the ice. We had to help push again. Eventually the wheel was freed and we proceeded on across. Finally, after four days of this kind of progress, we arrived at Tzitzehar."

During the first night on this bus trip, Jacob and Mary Janzen's baby died. (This family is our cousin's, our grandmother's nephew.) Early in the morning, they asked for and received permission to bury the body in a nearby burying ground. The ground was frozen, but the father, his older son, and Uncle John Block managed to dig a shallow grave and they placed the little body in its basket and buried it there in a strange land. God comforted the family, and we moved on. Our journey continued by bus toward our destination of Harbin. Unfortunately, we were on a bus that broke down. Two busses were to go on ahead and our bus had to stay behind to get repaired. They didn't promise to have the bus repaired in one day, so we had to stay in a smoky house. Mother relates, "Since I was pregnant and Mary was overdue, Henry Isaak came and said, 'You go on, you don't have much time.' We went on then and came to the hotel that was quite nice and we were able to rest for several hours.

"That was on Saturday that we arrived in Harbin. On Sunday, March 31, 1929, Mary was born. If we would have stayed behind, and Henry Isaaks had not changed places with us, then she would have been born in that smoky room on the muddy road." God intervened in a wonderful way for my parents.

"As we arrived at the train depot for our trip to Harbin, we were surprised to see the Russian flag flying side by side with the Chinese flag. We thought that we had left the Hammer and Sickle behind us forever, and here the flag was waving in the evening breeze. To our surprise, there were some Russian men working on the railroad. Later, we learned that this railroad was operated jointly by the soviets and Chinese. It had been built by the Russian tzar (whom most of us knew) with a ninety-nine year lease to use it. When the soviet revolution took place, the soviets negotiated with the Chinese to operate the Far Eastern Railroad on a fifty-fifty basis. Not only was the revenue to be divided fifty-fifty, but also the operating personnel. That meant that half of the personnel were soviets. For some unknown reason, we were assigned an entire railway car exclusively for our group (sixty-two persons) for the overnight trip to Harbin.

Life in China

ncle John related, "The City of Harbin, with a population of 760,000, was founded by the Russian tzar and was largely populated by Russian people. Since then, others had also come there to live. During the time of the Revolution, remnants of the White Russian army had fled to Harbin for safety. They were the army of the Republic, which was defeated by the Communists. They fled to Harbin and lived there and raised their families along with other refugees who had come over the years.

"The city had become a city of international residents. There were many Chinese shops and stores, but the larger businesses, like department stores and the city government, were run by Russians who had become Chinese citizens so they could legally remain even though they were Caucasian. Harbin was sort of like an international European city located right in the heart of Manchuria. There were Americans, British, Germans, and many other European descendants.

"When we arrived in Harbin, there were other people already there who were known to our parents. One was Henry Schmidt, who had lived with us for several years in Siberia. He was to have been drafted into the soviet armed forces, a circumstance he did not relish, and so just about the time for him to be inducted, he escaped into China and settled there. He had fled first to the Amur region together with his sister's family. They escaped across the river into China and came to Harbin just like our group did.

"The next day our men hurried out to find jobs. It was a surprise to us how fast they were able to find them. Some of our men found jobs on a construction project. It was heavy work, carrying buckets of concrete mix and sometimes wheeling around barrows of heavy wet concrete."

Heinrich and Anna circa 1929 when they left Russia.

Heinrich and Anna (Dad and Mom) celebrating their 25th Wedding Anniversary at Hubert and Katharine's Wedding October 21, 1949.

Wages were very low, so for a family man it was very difficult to make ends meet. My dad worked in a sausage factory for fifteen Tayan per month, which was not enough to pay the rent. Yet somehow our family got by. Other people worked at the plywood plant and other places that provided meager living, but God saw everyone through. During the entire time, delegated people such as John Friesen, George Klippen-stein, and John Isaak, along with others were diligently working on finding a way to immigrate to America.

Heinrich Rogalsky in 1929 family passport photo.

Margaret Friesen*, Anna, Katharine, Helen (above), Dad, Mary.
* Margaret Friesen's sister signed over temporary custody to my parents so that they could get her to the United States. She was 13 years old at the time.

We were told that Canada was closed and that there was no possibility of going there. Several of our men ventured out to see the United State Consulate. Although they did not really expect very much, they went to inquire about the possibilities of immigrating to the United States and were told no. The stock market had just crashed in 1929; there were long lines of the unemployed, and there were bread and soup lines in America. They did not need any more new people, and so they said there would be no possibility of getting to America.

Then our men told them that we were not labor people, we were agricultural people, we were farmers. Some of our people had managed to save some pictures of their farming operations. Everything that we had in the way of literature, maps, or pictures, except our Bibles, were confiscated and burned in the village of Tchekade where we waited to receive our Chinese passports. With the salvaged pictures, they made a new appeal to the United States.

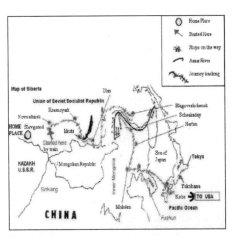

Map of our escape route from Russia to Japan and the United States.

Mother continues, "Helen had to go with me to see the eye doctor because we both had severe eye infections (trachoma) and the doctor was always so amazed that Helen never cried. She was easily amused. The nurse would give her two cotton balls to cover her eyes with, and that satisfied her completely. Because she never cried, they gave her a beautiful doll. This made Helen proud that she was the only girl to have such a beautiful doll. Whenever Helen went with me, I tried to take the bus or train, because she just couldn't walk that far, but when I went alone, I would walk, because it was to expensive to ride the train or bus. As serious as my eye infections were, my eyesight until recently has been perfect, as has Helens. She now wears glasses with bifocals. Dr. Isaak took such good care of us. We could not enter the US with any kinds of infection.

"Baby Mary had to go through a lot. Whenever I was gone she had to wait until I got back to feed her, and then I hardly ever had enough milk so we had to supplement her, and that was very difficult. Grandma had her often, and if Dad was home, then he would take care of her until I got home. Dad had to carry her a lot, because she often was hungry and therefore cried a lot.

"Our people also got in contact with the Mennonite leaders in the America. There was Reverend Daniel Eitzen of Reedley, California, and others who worked with their senators. Reverend Eitzen made several trips to Washington, D.C., and others wrote to their congressmen and senators asking them to allow these refugees to come to America."

Years later as my uncle John Block was writing his seminary thesis, he came across an article in a sociology magazine that reported that over two hundred people had come to the United States by special permission of congress. It described how we had come out of Russia into Harbin, China and on to the United States. That was a description of our group. It was then that he learned that it had actually taken a special act of congress to allow us entrance to the United States. It was actually an amendment attached to a farm bill in congress. It

These were our Chinese Passport covers.

happened during the time of President Herbert Hoover's administration. Vice President Curtis had made the decision since President Hoover was out of the country at the time. As a result of the prayer intercession and physical intercession by many people and our church leaders, we were given permission to immigrate to the United States.

We did not come to America by way of the regular quota, but by special permission as refugees without a country. We couldn't all come at once, because that would bring in a labor surplus and would, of necessity, cause some to rely on the State for assistance. They allowed us to come in groups of about fifteen people per month. Some months it was twelve people, and then other months it was sixteen people depending on the families. We were the last group to leave China.

We boarded the train in Harbin and went to the city of Mukden. That was the end of the Russian limit of the railroad. There we just walked through a little tunnel to board a train on the Japanese railroad to travel through Korea and on to the city of Fusan. There we boarded an overnight boat and crossed the Sea of Japan to get to Shimonisei, Japan.

From Shimonisei, we went by train to Kobe where we were to take a ship. My uncles and grandparents were the first group and they traveled on an American ship, the Lincoln Line, now known as the Presidents Line. We were the last group to leave China and we traveled on the SS Tenyo N.Y.K. Line voyage number 21. It took sixteen days to cross the Pacific on this ship from Kobe, Japan, to San Francisco.

On Our Way At Last

M other continues her story. "When we were ready to leave China for America, everyone had gotten a bus ticket to get to Japan except for us. Dad really scurried all over to try to get a spot and tickets for us on the bus to get to Japan. We were the last to get on the last bus to the station to Japan. We took a train to Kobe, Japan and we were there two days and one night. We took a little ship for one night and then we embarked onto the large ship and we were on it sixteen days. After two days, the captain told us that the weather would be stormy. The seasickness started. Dad was always on the deck. He was seasick, but he refused to stay below. He was better off on the deck. Mary was very sick, she was the baby and she stayed sick until we got to the United States. Most of the other passengers also were very sick. I stayed well and I didn't miss a meal. I took food from the table and ate it in the cabin, so I was able to gain the weight I needed to gain to pass the physical examination. The doctor ordered a glass of wine with each meal. When we arrived at the West Coast we were escorted to Angel Island on a small boat. Men and women with the children were taken to separate areas, but we could eat together. We stayed there one night. After all the physical examinations were finished, the Henry Isaaks had to stay behind. Henry Isaak's children's blood work indicated they had different mothers. So there was a question as to what had happened to the first wife. They were finally cleared. In China, all marriage licenses and papers had been confiscated. There were non-related people in our group who were able to validate the natural death and proper burial of Henry Isaak's first wife."

When we arrived in Reedley, we were well received. The people of the First Mennonite Church of Reedley had prepared a house and they had gathered clothes. We could pick and choose what we needed. We arrived on Saturday and we had to be in church on Sunday morning. What a sight we must have been. Reverend Henry Regier was the pastor and he was so good to us. We bought an old cow, chickens, and a setting hen. My dad had to work from noon until sundown. His hands were blistered from shoveling Bermuda grass for one setting hen. The pastor gave us our first sixteen setting eggs. Most of those eggs hatched. We kept the setting hens and butchered the little roosters. The first old cow did not bear anymore, so we butchered her and we canned the meat. We went to great pains to can the meat and dad gave the jars an extra tightening twist, which was the wrong thing to do because that broke the seal and all of the meat spoiled. We had a lot to learn.

Those first few years in the United States were very dif-ficult. Wages in those years were fifteen cents an hour and I remember my dad saying often, "If I didn't remember what we left, I'd go back, because life is so hard." However, he remembered what he had left, the denial of all personal freedom, the eradication of all teaching of God, and he knew he had made the right choice.

I am so thankful for the courage my mother and dad had to face those hardships of leaving and then the hard-ships of re-establishing their lives and striving for a better chance for their children.

My mother shared with me that early in the take over; the communists advocated free election or expressions of opinions. At the town meetings, women were encouraged to participate. Up until then women were not allowed to vote or speak out. So my dad was appointed to go to every household and tell the women to come to the town meet-ing. So, dad would go to every house and make the an-nouncement that there was to be a town meeting. All women were to come. Then he would say," But don't you dare come." Then the women who did not want to come anyway did not come. My dad had done his political duty, and the women had heard the announcement but took the right to refuse to come.

When we were all home together, we all worked very hard. Dad was a severe disciplinarian. The discipline and training has proven to be very good. Mother and Dad can be very thankful that they were faithful to the Lord in the way that they trained us. They gave us the opportunity to work and to learn to make the most of what we have. It was hard to feed nine of us when Dad was only earning fifteen to twenty-five cents per hour.

Dad finally got a job with Dan Kreibel. He would tell Dad, "Don't even think about the debt, your family comes first." However, Dad absolutely insisted that the first $25.00 from his paycheck would go toward the loan. Mr. Krehbiel would just shake his head and say, "Henry, I don't know how you do it."

Dad replied, "We have made a commitment and we intend to keep that. Our word is binding and we will take care of our debt before we do anything for ourselves."

Mother related, "When we made the last payment towards the loan, the George Klippensteins (also in that group) couldn't get over the fact that Dad, with his large family and being so very poor, had paid the loan off. Then he went about telling the others, 'Look at that, Henry has paid off his loan with his large family, and so many of you who have grown children who work still have not paid off that loan.' Then some were led astray by those who said why pay it off? That money was collected for that purpose and now the conference is asking us to pay.

"It was money that could be used by others trying to come to freedom. We understood that and agreed to that. We had no problem with that, however there are some of those people to this day who have prospered and have not repaid the debt. The total debt was $600.00, however the Nickels paid the share for Margaret. We still have the document of that agreement and the tallies of the payments and the dates of when and how much was paid."

Arriving in America

All of us that left Russia as a group and had been in China together did not all arrive in San Francisco. There was a division. Some of the people were to go to the state of Washington and others to California. An inter-Mennonite committee facilitated resettling of Mennonite people, particularly those from Russia.

It was this committee that also raised the money for us to come across the ocean. The money was given to us as a loan, not as a gift, which we repaid later. The committee members were the ones who were directing it. The settlers or the leaders of the group made the decision where each family would go.

Some families came to San Francisco to take the women with small children in their cars to Reedley. An Enns family took us and the Abe Klassen family who also had small children. We spent our first night a Saturday evening in the Enns' home. She was a lovely widowed lady who wanted to help. The next day they took us to church at the First Mennonite Church in Reedley and presented us to the congregation.

My grandparents, Uncle John, and Uncle Jacob arrived in Reedley before we did. The church had rented a big two-story house and provided food and dishes so that we could start our life there. We lived in the two story house for a short time with our grandparents, the Henry Isaaks and the Klassens. Then we rented the Neufeld's place on Columbia Avenue.

The Neufeld farm on Columbia Avenue had ten acres of seedless, Thomsen grapes. It was not a very productive crop-producing farm, but it was a place to live and to continue on with our lives. This farm was rented on a 60/40 percent share crop basis. The landowner received 60 percent of the income from the crop, and the renter received 40 percent of the income from the crop. That was not nearly enough money to live on so Dad worked on side jobs in the different food crops.

While we lived at the Neufeld's place I went to Lincoln School. In the summer months, it was so hot that we would move the wood cook-stove outside. We would cook outside under the large tree in the back yard.

I remember the water cooler that we used in the summer months. It was a wood-frame box covered with screen and burlap. The four feet were placed in tin cans of water to keep the ants away, and an empty gas tank was converted into a drip-tank that would drip water onto the burlap-covered box. A door was attached with hinges, and shelves were made in the box. That evaporative cooler was the way

Grandpa and Grandma Isaak.

we stored our milk, butter, watermelon, and other perishable foods in the summer months.

Then the depression got worse and worse and the payment for an hour's work was fifteen to twenty cents per hour. We were unable to continue to make regular payments on that loan. We had been promised that we would not be deported. However, the men would come around to see how we were doing and they would ask us, "Can you pay anything?" The answer always was "No, we can't this month."

The potato harvest in Shafter, California started in June, and since work around Reedley was slack at that time, most of the men and women able to work went to Shafter to work. My grandmother and grandfather who were

Grandma (Block) Isaak.

around sixty years of age were bending over picking up sack after sack of potatoes by hand all day long. Grandma was not very strong but she filled many sacks with potatoes. My father also worked in the potatoes and he became a sack sewer. When the hundred-pound sacks were full, he would sew them shut to prepare them for loading onto a trailer to be taken to market. My mother would stay home with us four little girls and do whatever was necessary on the farm, because dad was working long distances away from home.

On, March 1, 1931 my first little brother, Henry, was born. All five of my brothers were born at home. My parents became acquainted with Dr. Wiebe of Reedley, and when mother was pregnant Dad would notify the doctor who in turn would give counsel. When labor began my dad would notify the doctor and he and his wife, who was a well-trained nurse, would come to our house for the delivery.

My father's actual accounting for the contract.

I remember that my mother had arranged for us girls to spend the night with neighbors. The next day, I came home from school and there was mother in bed with a little baby brother. We were so excited. I asked where did he come from? My parents replied, "The doctor brought him in his big, black bag." He was our first brother and he was so very special to me. One special event I

Contracts that my father made when we arrived in the United States. (above and below)

remember so well, I was able to take my little brother to school one day for show-and-tell. He probably was around three years old and he was wearing green short pants. It was such an important day in my life and his as well.

Our living standard was lower than that of most the American people, and this served us well. Even though it was the depression for American people, it was a better time for us. Dad worked very hard and managed to save money, and every bit we saved was used to pay off our debt.

Dad worked in various crops, orchards, and fields. He even worked in the oranges in San Bernadino and Rialto for a time. Dad would leave for the orange orchards in Southern California and travel that narrow two-lane road through the grapevine on Highway 99, south of Bakersfield. He would come home to our family on alternate weekends during the orange picking season. Often Dad would say, "If I didn't know where I had come from I would return. This is so very hard."

Things were very difficult for us in those years. I was old enough to remember more than I do, but I cannot remember any clothes closets in our house. There was one tiny clothes-closet in our parents' bedroom. The Chinese people that had lived in the house before us had burned incense and the walls were saturated with incense smoke. We stripped the wallpaper and painted, and still the house smelled from incense, which we were not used to. We eventually built another bedroom onto the front porch.

My second brother, Frank, was born on July 28, 1932. Once again, we spent the night before his birth at the neighbor's house, the Dalkie family. And again, we asked the same question, "Where did the baby come from?" And we received the same answer, "The doctor brought him in his big, black bag." However, this time we actually saw the big, black bag because our baby brother was having some serious difficulty, and the doctor had to come to our house several times in one day. He and his wife worked on the baby for many hours. My parents were very anxious. Something was wrong with our brother Frank. He had what I now know as meconium ileus, which is an intestinal obstruction caused by the blocking of the bowels with the thick meconium. Dr. Wiebe and his wife worked hard most of the day with him and were finally able to relieve the obstruction, and our baby began to thrive.

Dad became a steady worker for Dan Krehbiel. The Neufelds place was sold and purchased by the Jake Gertz family and they really wanted us out of that house quickly. Dad looked for a place to rent but no one wanted to rent a house to such a large family. The Krehbiel place was going to be empty. The occupants, The Weinbrenners, wanted to go out on their own and were going to be moving. Dad wanted to rent that house but Mr. Krehbiel also was not sure of renting his house to such a large family. He was afraid that the children would be too destructive. Dad said, "Well I guess I'll just have to drown them all. I cannot find a place to live."

Mr. Krehbiel was shocked at that statement but did not give permission to rent. So dad watched, and as soon as Weinbrenners were moved out we moved in. Later on Mr. Krehbiel confessed he had been fearful at first, but later how thankful he was that we were living there because these children knew how to work and were obedient, productive, and respectful. Whenever he arrived on the property, the boys were right there to help and to pick up bad fruit. They were helpful in every way and the boys just won his heart. He gave us permission to pick and eat fruit from certain trees. We obeyed to the letter, he seldom criticized us or ever forbade us anything. There was one occasion, however, when one of my little brothers played with some of Mr. Krehbiel's tools and misplaced them. That upset him greatly, and my brothers received a stern warning not to do that again.

The school we attended was the Windsor School. I believe I was in the fifth-grade. John Berg was my teacher, and he taught a fourth and fifth-grade combined class.

On October 4, 1934 my brother John was born. He was the first child born on the Krehbiel place. My grandmother would come and stay in our home to help because my mother always had to stay in bed at least twelve to fourteen days after childbirth. Although I had a lot of responsibility, I was not able to do all that was required to care for the family needs, so my grandmother, and sometimes some of our aunts, would come and help out. I had to help with the smaller children and wash diapers with the scrub board every day after school.

Then on August 28, 1936 my brother Peter was born. John and Peter looked so much alike, they were often mistaken for twins.

During the summer months, we children and my mother would pick grapes and put them on trays to be made into raisins, and dad would go pick figs, because he could earn a lot more money picking figs than grapes. He taught us how to pick grapes, and the farmers loved to see us coming, because we knew what to do and we were not wasteful by dropping bunches of grapes on the ground. We worked hard and fast. Not much time for goofing off. Mother always had a baby under the vines in the shade while she worked with us in the fields. We put in long hours from about 7:00 A.M. until 6:00 P.M. every day with an hour or so for a lunch break. Sometimes, on terribly hot days, mother would allow us an extra half-hour to play in the shade. We were paid one cent per tray and sometimes one and a half cents per tray. On a good day I might cut 300 trays. The job hazard of picking grapes for raisins is that wasps just love to make their nests in the grapevines. When we would come upon a nest, they would dart out and sting us. I do not know of anything that hurts worse than a wasp sting. The way we handled that was, we would take one of the paper-trays, which were used for placing the grapes on, and roll it up and put a match to it and smoke the wasps away. Then we would quickly pick the grapes on those vines before the wasps would come back. We would put mud on the sting and continue with our work.

After Pete was born, Mother was sick a great deal of the time. I had to miss a lot of school. I learned to bake bread and to do all the necessary meal preparation chores on a wood-burning stove and oven. I also had to milk the cow and clean out the barn when necessary.

My mother was pregnant with my youngest brother. Now that I am an adult I realize that she had toxemia of pregnancy due to a tumor on her kidney. Doctor Wiebe did not know if she would survive the pregnancy, or the birth. My mother did survive the pregnancy, but the postpartum period was very serious. After the delivery, the doctor wanted to adopt our new baby brother in the worst way. They had never been blessed with a child of their own and they said to my parents, "You have such a large family and times are so hard, let us have this baby to raise as our own." My parents gave this serious consideration, and finally my mother said, "It appears that I may l not survive this, and, if that is the case, then you may have this baby. But as long as I have breath in my body, the baby will belong to us." Our baby brother, Nick, born on May 17, 1938, survived and is doing very well. My mother had to have a kidney removed after that birth, and that was a very critical time for our family. God was good, as He always is, and He showed mercy in allowing our mother to live and to see all her children grow up and to see most of her grandchildren and great grandchildren. She was 86 years old in 1990 when the Lord called her home. Dr. Wiebe and his wife both died years before my parents did.

We lived there until Krehbiels place was sold to Walt Krehbiel. We then rented a forty-acre farm owned by a Mrs. Smith near town, on Mallory Avenue. It was at that time that I went to Reedley High School. This place was for sale, and Dad tried to find money to make a down payment. He was dealing with a realtor, a man from our church, whom Dad trusted. He did not know that he had to put down earnest money. While he was out trying to find money, which he did, the realtor, called his friend to come and buy the land, which his friend did. When my father arrived with the money, the farm had been sold. My father was devastated that he was not able to have that farm. The owner of that land had really planned for my dad to buy that farm. The realtor had other plans. Then my father said this would never ever happen again. He would never trust anyone to borrow money. He would save until he had the cash in hand before he would attempt to buy land again.

It is somewhat ironic that after we moved away from that farm, the new owners asked my father to show them how he had irrigated the land. The vineyards had valleys and ridges, for the land was not flat, and Dad had devised ingenious ways to irrigate all segments of the vineyard. Dad decided to let the new owners solve that problem for themselves.

Life in America

We arrived in the United States at Angel Island on April 25, 1930. We left Russia on February 21, 1929. Fifteen months after we left Russia, we were in the United States of America. I remember very few incidents from the time we left to the time we arrived. One memory that comes to mind was as we were boarding the train in Russia. One of the men, I believe it was Henry Regehr, had me in his arms and took me onto the train. My father was carrying some bags and perhaps a child, I don't know, and Mother, being so very pregnant, had all she could do to manage the train step and get on the train herself. My other two sisters, Helen and Anna, were carried on by two of the young bachelors in the group.

While we were in China, I remember Margaret bringing me a Chinese wooden doll. Also, I remember drinking hot tea with milk and sugar in it. I remember seeing Chinese men sitting on the street corners smoking. I remember very little of our life in China. While on the ship traveling to the United States after leaving China, I recall that the seas were very rough. I had this horrible fear of falling down and rolling down the ship floor through the railing and into the ocean. Of course, that never happened, but the fear was very real to me. One time we had been ordered up to the deck from the dining area, and I was wearing a black apron, and we had eaten soft boiled eggs for breakfast, and I had spilled the yolk all over the front of it. Every one was sick, but I did not experience any sea sickness that I can recall.

When we arrived at Angel Island, we were separated from our dad. The children and the women were segregated to one section, and the men to another, for physical examinations. We had to give them urine specimens, stool specimens, and were examined by the medical personnel. When all of that was finished, we were allowed to go to San Francisco where we were met by many people with private cars and a truck for our transportation to our new home in Reedley, California. My mother traveled in a car because she had a little baby my youngest sister, Mary and Anna. Dad, I, and Helen were in the back of a truck. That was certainly a new experience for all of us. I remember so well observing the beautiful countryside with all the trees leafing out and the grapevines leafing out. My dad asked someone what those little funny trees were, and he was told they were grapevines.

We purchased a car from a Mr. Suderman, who had a used car garage, and we purchased the best car of all the others who purchased cars. It was a Model T Ford with celluloid windows and four doors. They purchased a license for Dad and showed him how the car operated and told him to drive, and he did. No big drivers-test. Dad was a good driver.

When we arrived in Reedley, we were taken to a two story house, and three families were going to be staying here until further arrangements could be made for our lodging.

The house had been stocked with bedding and kitchen utensils and some food to help us get started. We also were provided with some clothes, because we had very little with us. The people were very kind to us. My mother tells me that we had to get ready for church the next day, because everyone wanted to meet us. We were bathed and dressed in the clothes that had been provided for us and went to church the next morning. We all sat in one pew and were very quiet and very good.

We then were moved to another house, which was on Columbia Avenue. That was our first residence in Reedley. The Neufeld ten-acre grape farm. We had a two bedroom frame house, with a deep water well under the house. That was our water source and we had a hand-pump with a sink in the kitchen, where we got all of the water for all of our household use. The house also had a kitchen combination dining room. It had an outhouse. Our dining room had a large table and two benches on either side of the table, where we children sat, and Mother and Dad each had a chair at either end of the table. We all had our own plate. Each plate had a different pattern. So we always had our own special plate. We drank out of a communal large, blue enamel cup, which was placed in the middle of the table. Of course, we had flatware that had been provided for us in our first house. I do not recall closets or dressers or where we put our clothes. I know that I had a Sunday dress and a dress for everyday.

We heated our water for bathing and laundry in a large twenty-one-gallon caldron that was located outside. Dad made a metal frame for it to rest upon, and underneath it we would build a wood fire. When the water was hot, we would carry it with buckets into the house and pour it into galvanized tubs in which we bathed every Saturday night. We also made all of our own soap in that caldron and boiled laundry in it. The caldron had many other uses.

I do not remember very much about those first few months except that we were getting acquainted with life in the United States.

We socialized with our relatives. We would get together at my grandmothers house at least every two weeks on a Sunday afternoon, and we would play many outdoor games together. We would play run sheep run, kick the can, hide and seek, and many other games. We would be anywhere from ten to twenty children ranging in age from infants to adolescents. We developed very close family ties in this manner. We would always eat together around 5:00 P.M. Our meal would consist of sweiback, which is a special home baked roll, cold cuts, sliced cheese, with mustard and butter. We also would have home baked pastries and sometimes canned fruit. The men would be served first, then the women, and then the children. The dishes would all be washed before we left my grandmothers house. The men would sit in the front parlor, also known as the Sunday room, and talk about their war stories and what they had left behind, and crack sunflower seeds. The women would take care of the children and prepare for the supper as well as visit about their concerns and what their lives were like in this new environment.

We would meet in various homes at least every two weeks. I have always been so grateful for this experience because I know all of my cousins, and we had a very close relationship over the years. That was a very necessary part of our survival in this new country.

The doors and windows were always open in the summer time because it was so hot and the only cooling we could get was the outside air. Dad would move the kitchen cookstove out of the house every summer, and we would cook outside under a shade tree. It was just too hot to bake bread and to cook on our wood-burning stove in the summer time.

After a few years, we were able to use a kerosene stove for cooking in the summer, but we had to buy the kerosene for that. It was too costly to burn all winter. The wood was available for free, and in the winter months we needed the heat from the stove so we would cook and bake again with the wood-burning stove.

I learned to bake bread by the time I was twelve or thirteen years old. Mother was very sick much of the time during those years, so I had to learn to do the basics because my dad certainly could not stay home. Mother taught me well. I could tell by putting my hand into the oven to check the temperature and know when to put the bread or cake or whatever I was baking into the oven. I don't remember having any failures as far as the baking was concerned. If there were any, we ate it anyway.

After a few years, Mr. Kreihbel gave us his old icebox to use instead of the burlap cooler. We were so thrilled. Now the ice man would deliver a fifty pound ice block several times a week so that we could store our perishable foods safer and better.

Every fall there would be a day set aside for butchering. All of the families would get together for this day of butchering. Usually my grandparents would come along with some of my uncles and aunts and their children. That was always a festive big event. The men would do the actual killing of heifer or pig (whichever it would be) and then they would dress out the animal. My dad was very good at dressing out the animals, making the sausage, and cutting the meat. The pig butchering was more involved than the heifer butchering. With the pig, there were intestines to clean for use as sausage casing. Also, to clean the pig's feet, ears, tongue, snout, for pickling, and to make headcheese. We also made liverwurst and spareribs. Those would be cooked the very same day and would be enjoyed for dinner that night and shared with all who came to help. The lard was rendered in the big twenty-one gallon caldron that we normally used for our hot water supply. The liverwurst and spareribs were cooked in the fat that was being rendered for crackling lard and greveschmalt, which was used as a bread spread instead of butter.

Regarding the cleaning of the pig intestine, that chore was my grandmother,s responsibility. She was a master at this. The intestines were all turned inside out and washed with cornmeal mixture and rinsed. Then she would take a pair of thin knitting needles and run the intestines between them and clean off the mucous membrane lining, which was done neatly and without tearing the casings. They were thoroughly cleaned and ready for sausage use and for the liverwurst. Butchering day was always a joyous, happy, social event.

Every year, when our cow would be dry because of carrying a calf, we would have our milk delivered by a milkwagon. This wagon was pulled by one horse, and we would buy buttermilk and sweet milk from that vendor. We would hear him coming and we would wait out by the road with our container, and he would fill it up for us. Then we would pay him for it, and that was how we bought our fresh milk in those days.

The first farm we lived on was the Neufeld's place. It was sad. All we had was one almond tree for shade. One year all of the leaves had fallen off because of some insect that had infested the tree. On another occasion, we had gone visiting to the Isaaks and when we returned home our floor was covered with a thick layer of ants. What were we to do? We hand pumped water into the buckets and poured the water on the ants and swept them out with the broom so that we could enter the house. The house had a deep well and we hand pumped all the water we used. Sometimes the water would not come up, and Dad would have to go down the ladder to the well and prime the pump so that the water would come up the pipe. Those were scary days for me. I had such a fear of falling into that well, although we had a hinged trap door on it so dad could go down when he had to prime the pump or whatever.

The first year we had that farm we had a crop failure due to lack of rain. The second year was better, and the third year we were able to rent the Krehbiel house, and Dad worked for him and others. We purchased the first washing machine with a wringer and with two rinsing tubs while we lived at the Krehbiel house. John was a baby. That was in 1934. Up until then, we had to hand wash all the clothes on an anchor-glass scrub board.

My dad applied for United States citizenship papers. We had to wait two years before we could apply for citizenship. Then we had to wait another five years to make a second application. Miss Lindberg was the teacher in the ESL night school where Dad attended the class. She was so patient with Dad to teach him how to read and to make the correct pronunciation. He went to school seven years to learn English and learn the Constitution of the United States. Mother could not go to school at that time. After Dad got his citizen papers in 1938, he said, "Now it will be your turn." We four girls derived our citizenship with Dad's citizenship acceptance.

In 1940, Mother took her test and passed with flying-colors. The judge was so taken by her knowledge of the constitution and the way she spoke that he just talked with her for the joy of hearing her responses. Mother learned to read from reading our schoolbooks. When we brought them home, I helped her with the reading and pronunciation.

Then she went to the adult night school to study the constitution and to memorize all of the amendments, which was required to take the citizen ship examination.

Going
to School

I really don't know how my father registered us for school. He told us that he had spoken with the teachers, and we had better be good, or else. I assure you, I was the best I knew how. He also told me that I had to write with my right-hand. I was left-handed. I believe the teacher tried to make me change, but to no avail. She did do something very special for me, since I was insisting on writing with my left-hand she taught me to turn my paper for left-handed writing and not for right-handed writing, which proved to be of great benefit for all of my school adventure. I do not write upside down as do so many left-handed people.

My first year of school was very difficult. My teacher, Miss Sharton, assigned a disadvantaged red-haired girl to be my mentor because she also spoke the German dialect that I speak, and, therefore, she was supposed to be of valuable assistance. She was very mean to me and pinched me

Helen, Frank, Mary, John, Ann (up), Henry (wagon) and Katharine. My Dad got the best bargain of all the men on his first car purchase—it was a Model T Ford.

until my arms were black and blue. That was so difficult for me. My parents have told me that I never cried because I had to go to school, but that I cried because I was so mistreated, and there was not much they could do, because of the language difficulty. Also, there was no time to go and talk to the teachers. Often, my lunch would be stolen and thrown away. Mr. Ramsey, the school custodian, would find me crying because I could not find my lunch sack and he would take me to the furnace room and share his lunch or get a bowl of soup from the school cafeteria for me. I will always remember the kindness that gentle school custodian showed me. He would find my lunches behind the baseball diamonds and wherever my tormentors had thrown them out. It took me two years to finish the first-grade.

During that time my mother gave birth to our first little brother, Henry, so that meant that when I came home from school there were diapers for me to wash, along with my other household chores.

During my second year at school, I was assigned to a combination-class, and I had a very kind teacher, Mrs. Linschied, who really knew how to help me. I so well remember coming home and teaching my sisters what I had learned. We would have a classroom outside, and the sideboard of our house was my blackboard, and the charcoal from the wood-burning stove was my chalk. I would write on the side of the house the words I had learned, and we played school more than any other game. I was determined to help my sisters know more than I did when I started school so that they would not have such a difficult time. That proved to be good for them because they did not endure the abuse I had.

I did well in the combination-class and was subsequently promoted to the third-grade and, once again, caught up with my age-level classmates.

My third-grade teacher was a Miss Carlson. She was very nice and helpful and a great support to me. I did not have many friends at school. I usually had to hurry home from school because there were many chores for me to do and I had to help my mother as soon as I got home. I had to help take care of my younger siblings. At about age nine or ten, I began to grow very fast, which was a little alarming. I was so much bigger than any one else in my age group. I was about eight inches taller than my sister Helen who was fourteen months younger than me. Mother said they were quite concerned, but felt it best just to wait this growing spurt out and see what would happen. By the time I was thirteen years old, I did not grow any more and I was the tallest person in the family until my brothers grew up.

When I was in the fourth-grade, the teachers were finally convinced that I could not see. They called attention to that by notifying the school nurse. Her name was Mrs.

Isaak. She made several calls on our home trying to convince my dad that he needed to sign a release form so that the Lions Club could provide glasses for me. My father was very fearful of signing any kind of document, because in Russia, it was the signed documents that put many people in slave-labor camps. My father had an on going fear of somehow being betrayed and returned to Russia if he signed any kind of document. It took Mrs. Isaak many months to convince my dad that no harm would come to him. He finally decided he would take the risk and sign the permission slip for the Lions Club to provide much needed glasses for me. The Lions Club provided my glasses for me through twelve grades of school. That was a wonderful provision for me. I could finally see the blackboard, and my studying became easier and I did so much better in school. I have continued to be grateful for the kindness and perseverance of Mrs. Isaak to not get discouraged and to follow through on the much needed glasses for me. She became my model as I later entered nurses training and completed that course successfully. I understand that the Lions Club to this day continues to provide glasses for the needy children in our schools. What a marvelous service that is.

We went to the First Mennonite Church every Sunday. We always went to Sunday school. Our parents also went to Sunday school because it was conducted in German. We never stayed for church because it was in English and we could not understand the service. I used to memorize the Bible verses and win most of the contests that were held. I loved to be in Sunday school and learn the Bible stories. I had a wonderful junior department teacher. Her name was Mrs. Enns. She was a godly role model for me. I had a deep hunger to know spiritual truth. Whenever there was a revival meeting in town, I would try to attend. I was so eager to learn all that I could about what a personal relationship with Jesus was all about.

We moved from the Columbia Avenue place to the Krehbiel place, and there we went to Windsor Elementary School. It was a red brick school house (one of the few remaining school houses in the country by the same architect). That school was a country school, and almost all of the classes were combination-classes. I was in the fourth/fifth-grade combination-class. Mr. John Berg was my teacher, and being that this community was strong with Mennonite Brethren people, most of the kids and many of the teachers were Mennonite Brethren. We rode a bus to school and we met the bus at a crossroad near our home.

Our immediate neighbors were John and Lois Gerbrandt. They had two boys, John and Marvin, and a girl, Lois. Mr. Gerbrandt was a pastor in a small community church of Navelencia, and it was through their testimony and their interest in our family that I was saved while in the eighth-grade. A pastor, Reverend George Milton Towle, an artist evangelist, held a week of meetings. On the last night of those meetings I made a definite decision for Jesus. That pastor took the time to explain the difference between faith and feelings, and I was able to apply that truth to my life. Then as I entered high school. John Strain, who was the vice-principal, took it upon himself to disciple me. I have always been grateful for that, because as a result of that discipling process and Christian Bible studies on the campus, I came to an understanding of the personal relationship God wants to have with His children. I was His child, and I eagerly wanted to grow in my Christian walk.

Treasure Island

In 1939, I had the privilege of attending the 1939 World Exposition held on Treasure Island in San Francisco. My father had gone. When he came home he said one of his children must go to this great, wonderful fair. I don't remember the circumstances of my father being able to go to the exposition, but he told me that if I could somehow arrange to go to the fair for ten dollars, I could go. Ten dollars was a lot of money.

The high school announced that a package was available for ten dollars. It included a roundtrip ticket on the train plus the ferry ride and an admission ticket to the fair. A twenty-four hour trip. I was able to go. My mother packed a lunch for me in a large, paper grocery bag (enough food for a week, I'm sure). When I arrived at the train depot in Reedley, I had no special friend to go with, so I attached myself to a couple, Mr. and Mrs. Walter Krehbiel, from my church so that I would not get lost. When I got to the Treasure Island Fair site, I felt that the Kreihbiels really didn't want me tagging along so I attached my self to a pair of maiden ladies and soon discovered that they were to slow for me. I wanted to see everything, and so I stashed my lunch in one of the restrooms as I entered the fair grounds and then I took off on my own. I saw everything. It was the most exciting day in my entire life. My dad had told me some of the important things I should see, and I did see everything he told me I should. They were very special indeed, things like the *Cavalcade of the Golden West*, a movie production of how the west was discovered. I watched my time to be at the exit gate by 9:00 P.M. to catch the ferry and then catch the train for home. There, once again, I met with the Walter Krehbiels, and I sat by them on the way home. I had retrieved my lunch at the end of the day from the restroom where I had left it and I probably ate something, I don't remember. I know I was too busy seeing everything to eat during the day. What a marvelous experience, and all for ten dollars.

Years of 1941–43

Those were the war years and there was much unrest in the world. Then on December 7, 1941, I was a sophomore in high school, Pearl Harbor took place, and our lives changed. In the late 30's, while the war against communism was being waged by Hitler against Russia, there was much political discussion in our household about the war and wanting to see deliverance from the perils of communism for my many relatives that were still in Russia.

Then in 1941, when we were involved in the war by Japan attacking the US at Pearl Harbor, many more things changed in our lives. Many of my classmates enlisted or were drafted into military service. Many of my dearest friends and our neighbors were Japanese, and they were all interned to areas in the Midwest that had been established as safe places for them during the war. Most of the friends I had during that time, I lost track of and have seen only a few at subsequent high school reunions. Some of my classmates were killed in the war. One I remember so well was our neighbor as well as a good friend of our family, Stanley Hongola. His parents had immigrated from Finland just before we came to America, and he had a younger brother, Norman, and an older brother, Russell, who later became a doctor and he treated my father when he became ill.

I was working in the high school cafeteria for Mrs. Miller, and she taught me how to cook. She asked me if I would like to cook breakfast for the signal corps men who were stationed in Reedley at the time. That meant that I had to be in the cafeteria around 5:30 A.M., and since we lived just outside of Chinatown, it was not deemed safe for me to ride my bicycle through town in those early hours. So, the local sheriff came to my house in his patrol car every morning and took me to school so that I could prepare breakfast for the signal corps men. I did that job until I graduated from high school and then the signal corps was sent to another area.

All during my high school years, I worked for Mrs. Miller in the cafeteria. I worked during my study hall period, which was in the morning. At that time, I would prepare salads, cook hot dogs, and fry hamburgers. Sometimes I would fry as may as twelve dozen hamburgers to be served during lunch hour. Then I worked the noon hour to serve the meals to the students. I got paid for the study hall period and I received my lunch for the noon hour work. She really had confidence in me, so she asked me to help her whenever she had to put on a banquet for one of the organizations in town, or other special occasions. I learned so much from her. I worked for her until I left town to go on to further schooling.

During my high school years, I worked very hard on the farm, as well as my classroom studies. I helped my dad prune grapes every winter, and in the spring and fall to shovel Bermuda grass, that pesky and difficult to destroy grass in the vineyards. I also swamped boxes when the grapes were harvested for the winery. That was very hard, backbreaking work. I worked like a man would during those years.

During the summer months, I picked grapes or packed fruit in the packing sheds. We never were idle and we worked long hard hours.

The one pleasure I remember was a band concert at our local park on Thursday evenings. We went every Thursday evening with our quilts and sat on the grass and enjoyed the concert along with being able to play around with some of our friends.

Another memory comes to mind. During the summer before I started into high school, I had an emergency appendectomy. My nurse, Mrs. Isaac, who was the public-health nurse who had visited our home many times in the early elementary school years, took care of me. It was because of her example to me that I decided to become a nurse.

While I was recovering, my Sunday school teacher decided to give me a surprise birthday party in the park. That was my very first birthday party ever and was very special to me.

I worked as a volunteer nurse's aide for a few years while I was in high school. Those were the years when the candy stripers were still able to give care such as back rubs. Those were wonderful experiences for me and helped me to form some long-term goals for my life.

I remember several incidents on the Krehbiel farm. There was an electric water-pump in the yard near the house.

The pump was run to fill the storage tank for the water we used in our house. One day, while the pump was in operation, my little brother Peter was watching the gears mesh together in the operation of the pump, and he was so fascinated that he stuck his finger into the gears, and the first joint of his finger was ground into the gears. We had to rush him to the doctor's office for a quick repair and bandage. It is amazing to me that with our large family and all of us being so young and having so much responsibility that we did not have more accidents. We all survived pretty well. I remember there were times that I had to help Dad drive the team of workhorses with the plow in the fields. My dad usually did this, but there were times when I had to drive the team. That was always a terrifying experience for me because I always was afraid of the horses. They were not our pets, however, they were gentle horses, but we did not ride them.

I learned to milk the cow, and that was one of my daily chores morning and evening. There were times when I had to milk two cows every morning before going to school. That was the time that I would practice my singing, and I enjoyed singing a great deal. While I was milking her, the cow would always swish me with her tail trying to shoo the flies off her back. She did not kick the bucket over very often. I learned well how to handle her and the bucket so that this would not happen. We had a milk separator in our house, and after I milked the cow, we poured the fresh milk through a cheesecloth strainer into the separator, and we cranked the handle, which started a centrifuge process, and the milk was separated from the cream. The cream was chilled and aged for a few days before it was churned into butter. We drank the milk, and we also made cottage cheese. We had many kinds of milk soup and buttermilk soup and clabbered milk, known today as yogurt, and what was left over was given to the pigs. Nothing was ever wasted.

During my high school days, I held many jobs. Dr. and Mrs. Trabor hired me to work for them. She felt that a farm girl would know how to work, and she was not disappointed. She taught me how to iron white shirts, serve guests, polish silverware, clean tile bathrooms with a toothbrush, iron linen tablecloths, and dress and cut up chickens. She had many social events in her home that I had to prepare for and clean up after. She taught me many social skills, which were invaluable to me.

All during my elementary school days and on into high school, I had a draining ear. We had gotten some medical care for it, but were never able to get the draining stopped. I had a very difficult time hearing as well, and since I did not see well, I always had a front seat so the loss of hearing was not a major concern for me, but the draining ear was. When I was working for Dr. Trabor, he finally was able to tell me how to treat it and healed my draining ear problem. He told me to put ten drops of rubbing alcohol into my ear several times a day. The pain was excruciating because my ear was so sore but I had to stop the draining. It worked. It took several weeks but it cleared up and my ear drum healed. I have very limited hearing in my left ear as a result of that longtime infection. I had many ear infections as a child, and my father would blow smoke into my ear, and that would relieve the pain, as well as a few drops of warm olive oil instilled into my ear by my mother.

I worked very hard for Mrs. Trabor for fifty cents a day. She was sad when I had to stop working for her during the summer months to help my parents in the vineyards. That paid more than fifty cents a day and times were hard.

I did live-in babysitting where I cooked for the family and took total care of the children while the mother worked. I also worked as a chambermaid in the local hotel. That did not last long, only a few months. But I learned to make beds very well.

I babysat for the junior college president and his wife. They totally trusted me as a high schooler to care for their three children while they went out or away for weekends. I did the laundry, cleaned the house, and watched the children. By today's standards for babysitters, I was quite a bargain for the families I worked for.

23

Academics

When I was in the seventh-grade, I took up playing the clarinet. I was in the school band and I was so proud to be able to play an instrument and to march in the band.

I also was a teachers aide and I assisted the teachers with getting their mimeograph material done for classroom assignments and was a general help in grading papers.

When I reflect on those events, I am filled with admiration for my parents and gratitude to God for His sustaining grace. I'm not sure that they had any idea of all the extra things I did while in school during the day. I never stayed after school. I needed to get home, there was a lot to be done. I had to study after school, of course, but that came after the chores were done. I had to learn to organize my life and my parents were the models of that for me.

After graduation from the eighth-grade, I had dreams of going on to high school. I had looked forward to this broadening of my horizons, however, my parents had other plans for me. Because I was the oldest member of the family and also because I was a girl, high school was not in the plans for my life as far as my parents were concerned. They knew by law I had to remain in school until I was sixteen and then I would be released to go to work and help provide towards the family income. Their plan for me was to go to work for some wealthy family as a housekeeper or live in nanny and thereby provide extra income for our large family. Dad was the only breadwinner except for the summer time when we all worked in the harvest fields. They had planned for me to go two years to the local church-school, which would fulfill the legal requirements of being in school until I was sixteen, and then I would be free to work. That entire summer after graduation from the eighth-grade, I begged my father to allow me to go to school. I promised to do anything, just so I could go to school. After coming home from work, I begged daily to be allowed to go to high school after the summer season was over. I always received no as the answer. I was a girl and I did not need an education. Then on the day of registration, my last chance, I begged my father again to allow me to register and go to school. After presenting me with a list of requirements I had to meet, he said he would allow me to try. I was able to register, and my life in the Reedley High School began. I have always been grateful and continue to be grateful for the way the Lord softened my father's heart to allow me to go to school.

When I was in high school, I held many jobs to be able to continue in school. I had to study after my siblings went to bed. We were living in a two bedroom house, and the only place to study was at the dining-room table, and that would not be free to use until everyone had gone to bed. So, I was usually up quite late getting my homework done. I never resented that because I was so glad to be able to be going to school. I was on the debating team, and Mrs. Evans, the teacher-sponsor in that program, was very helpful to me. I really was a country bumpkin and did not know any of the social graces. She encouraged me so much, and I enjoyed the debating team. I learned self-confidence and learned to express myself in a way that I had not experienced in life before.

I also was a participant in an Indian club drill team. The clubs looked like bowling ball pins and they had gas wicks on the ends and they would be lighted at night when the drill team would perform, and we would twirl and spin those clubs to music and made the most spectacular fiery designs. We were always applauded into encores. I thoroughly enjoyed that drill team for an entire school year.

I always will be grateful for vice principal of the school, Mr. John Strain, for taking me under his wing for the purpose of discipleship in my early Christian life. He was responsible for sponsoring me for several Christian camps. He taught me biblical truth in the lunchtime Bible studies, which he had invited me to, and which included junior college students and some high school students. Because of his influence in my life, I made the decision to further my education by going on to the Bible Institute of Los Angeles for three years to get a good Bible foundation for my life.

That is where my life really began as far as my spiritual journey is concerned. I am continually reminded in Scripture to tell the children so that they will not forget to remember how God has been faithful. So I feel compelled to include my spiritual journey in this document so those who will read this in future years will remember and see God's faithfulness in all areas of my life. But for the grace of God in my life, none of this is important to remember or even talk about.

24
Reminiscing

I asked my siblings to contribute what they remembered about our early life in the United States. Being the eldest in the family, I probably remembered more than they did, and they said they just could not remember anything significant. However, two of them did contribute their thoughts about what they remembered, and I felt it would be very beneficial to include their remarks in this chapter. My sister Helen, who is a year younger and the second member of the family and also born in Russia, and my brother Peter, who is the eighth member of the family and born in the United States, contributed, and I will submit their thoughts in this chapter.

Helen Remembers

"My first memories are living on Columbia Avenue. I remember the hot summers. We shooed flies out of the house with Mom's used aprons and tea towels, and cooled the house off by hosing down the floors with water.

"I used to sit under a tree near the road and listen to the radio in the house across the street. Then there was the year that the worms or caterpillars were eating the foliage off of the grapevines. We had to pick off those ugly caterpillars and squash them.

"One day, I decided to help the neighbors by taking the mail out of their box and taking it to them. They explained to me that it was against the law, and that has stuck with me. I never did it again. My first-grade teacher was Miss Sharton, and she was very nice, but I cried and wanted to go home. She put my lunch up high on the shelf in the coat closet and I stayed. I couldn't leave without my lunch.

"I remember our neighbors, the Dalkies. I would go help them separate milk and eat that warm foam. In order to play with the Firsicks, our other neighbors, we usually had to help someone do the dishes first.

"The Hongolas's were the neighbors across the street from us and they were also immigrants from Finland. They were very good to us. Russell, Stanley, and Norman were the three brothers. Russell later became a doctor, Stanley died in World War II, and Norman was the youngest.

"Then we moved out on Reed Avenue and went to Windsor School. Mr. Berg was such a good man and teacher. Some of the kids made fun of us and sometimes it was very hard. The Gerbrandts were wonderful neighbors. We had to work very hard in the summers, and sometimes Mom was very sick.

"We cut yellow peaches for drying at Ben Fast's house. They lived on the river bottom, and the owner of their home was the same Dan Krehbiel that owned the house we lived in. It was a dirty job, but thinking back now, that variety of peach is no longer in existence, but it was the best peach for drying.

"Also we cut grapes for drying and had to make a nice full tray. The Richert ladies, Agnes and Susie, were so good to us and always praised us for the good work we did and brought us cookies to eat at break times.

"We also went to German Bible school for six week sessions every summer for several years. We learned to read and write German and also learned Bible stories in German.

"I helped Mrs. Mierau in her home while she was ill. She had a little four or five year old boy, Bob. I learned a lot from her about cooking and taking care of Bob. He is now a commercial pilot and farms out near Windsor School. He has a lovely wife and two daughters.

"We moved back to town, and I finished the second half of the eighth-grade at Grant School. It was a real good change because I found out what poor teachers we had at Windsor and I learned a lot at Grant. It gave me a much better start for high school.

"I wore my first pair of nylons (or rayon) stockings at General Grant School graduation.

"We were always very crowded in our bedrooms at home. I remember when we built two bedrooms onto the front of the house on Mallory Avenue (Frankwood now) and Katharine, and I had one and Ann and Mary had one. The five brothers all shared one bedroom.

"I remember having the mumps real bad along with Henry, and we had to stay home from the Sunday school picnic at Mooneys Grove Park in Visalia.

"I remember when Dad was able to buy his own place, twenty acres of rundown vines on Parlier Ave. He really worked hard and improved it much even the first year.

"I think I enjoyed high school. I worked in the cafeteria for thirty-five cents per hour so I could buy fabric and supplies for my sewing class. I also enjoyed working at Nash De Camp packing house and was one of the fastest fruit packers. I enjoyed my friends Lena and Elvina, but they always seemed to have more money than I did. I don't know how much that bothered me?

"I remember going to church on Sundays and fussing because the boys were not supposed to sit on our laps and wrinkle our dresses (so they stood until they got too tall to stand in the car. We took up an entire pew at church and we had to behave.

"One Sunday, soon after I got my license to drive (my boy friend taught me), Dad had to stay home and watch the irrigation so he said for me to take everyone to church. When I parked at church, it was on a slight incline so I put on the emergency brake. When I went home I forgot about the brakes and they started smelling hot. I was so scared. Henry remembered the brakes, so we stopped and got out of the car. A man stopped and asked if he could help, so he looked at them and said it was OK to go home. Then I was afraid to tell Dad. When he found out, he was only mad because I had not told him. Driving could have been dangerous with bad or no brakes!

"I remember the Easter sunrise services, Dad used to take us up on the hill. It was really special.

At home we sat on benches on both sides of the table. We had one blue, large enamel cup for water. That cup got passed around to anyone who wanted a drink during the meal. Mom would put the meat onto our plates, and Dad would always get his first. It was proper.

"We had a great time with the cousins at our grandparent's house on Sunday afternoons. I remember sliding down the hills on Reed Avenue. At the Faspa of zwieback and cheese and baloney, the men were always served first, then the children were served last. The women usually ate after the men, except for the ones who were taking care of little children or serving the meal."

Pete Remembers

"The first memories of my childhood are of the Ennses place in Reedley. That is the house on Mallory Avenue. I can recall the house and the barn where we had our cow. There also was another barn-garage combination where we kept our tractor and other farm implements. I don't remember much of that place, except it was a large farm with grapevines of more than one variety. I know that muscats were part of the grape vineyard. We boys liked to play around the pump house, and one day John climbed up on the roof, jumped off, and broke his arm. Dr. Schlichting did a good job of setting the bone and splinting him, because he healed without any lasting difficulties. I thought for a long time that was why he was left-handed because he couldn't use his right hand due to the broken arm.

"I have vague recollections of some of our Japanese neighbors having to leave due to the relocation program during WWII. I remember the sadness of seeing so many fine families and friends being forced from their homes and loaded onto trains to be transported to the relocation centers. As time goes on, I realize more and more the wrong that was done to many fine and loyal Americans.

"I started first-grade at Washington School in Reedley. We Rogalskys apparently didn't think kindergarten was necessary, because none of us were enrolled in kindergarten. We all were bilingual as we grew up speaking Low German at home to Mom and Dad and English to each other. I realize today, more than then, the advantages we had in being able to speak two languages. When I was in high school and took German as a foreign language, it came very easy, and as a result got good grades. Several boys I started school with continue to be good friends, as we went to church together and also went through high school together. We have maintained contact with each other since that time. Roland Bergthold, David Krehbiel, and William (Willy) Buckley continue to be good friends of mine.

"When I was in second-grade, about Christmas time, we moved to our farm on Parlier Avenue. This was the farm that the folks bought, and we were all proud to have our own place. Little did we know, at the time, of the poor condition of that farm and the hard work it would require of all of us to make it produce. Four of us enrolled in Alta School, Frank, John, Nick, and myself. Henry finished his eighth-grade year at General Grant School in Reedley.

"Alta School was a two room schoolhouse, and, as a result, more than one Rogalsky was in the same room most of the time. There weren't many misdeeds that didn't get reported at home with a brother in the same room. I remember Mrs. Eva Stay as my first teacher there. She also was the principal. Miss Verna Jensen was my upper-grade teacher from the fifth-grade through the eighth-grades. I believe Mrs. Stay started me on my career as a school teacher. As a fourth-grader, the oldest level in her room, I was asked to help the first-graders with their reading. I remember reading with them in the reading circle. This may have had a profound influence on my decision to pursue a teaching credential at the college level.

"Our farm was twenty acres of Thompson seedless grapes on sandy soil. We had three acres of open land in the southwest corner of farm, where various crops were raised. Alfalfa was the most long-standing crop we had on that piece of ground before we planted it with grapevines. An irrigation ditch cut through the northwestern most corner of the farm. This ditch served as our swimming pool as we were growing up. The cemented drop provided a pool of clean water to swim in on most summer days.

"We made many improvements on the farm, and the one that I remember most vividly was laying a pipeline along the

western end of the vineyard. We dug the trench by hand, with each of us digging the depth of one shovel. Five of us dug, one behind the other with Dad finishing up the sides and bottom of the trench. With the

Dad and Mom—circa 1950.

trench dug, the pipe laying was done next. We lifted each thirty-six inch section of cement pipe into the trench, and Dad applied the cement to seal the joints. When all was finished we

had a modern irrigation system for the entire twenty-acre farm. While growing up, I hated farm work and regarded it as something we were required to do but didn't have to like it. I didn't appreciate the value of hard and diligent work until I assumed

Our first house, 1944.

some responsibility for the farm operation after Dad died in 1960. After that, I began to actually enjoy some of the work that had to be done. However, pruning the grapevines continued to be drudgery, since it is a slow and tedious task.

"We were a sports-minded family, with the girls, all older than the boys, participating in GAA in high school. All the boys in the family participated in sports while in high school. We all played basketball and were all on the starting lineup of one team or another while we were in high school. We had a basketball net in the back yard and had some real ball games after school and on weekends. Allowing us to participate in sports was a major concession for the folks because it took us away from working the farm during the sports season. Basketball was permitted readily because it was played in the winter and not too much could be done after school. Although we were on basketball teams, none of our chores were allowed to go undone. The cows had to be milked twice daily, and all the farm animals fed at the proper times. Pruning and tying the grapevines was done on Saturdays. Of course, Dad worked all week long making sure the work was done on time. Tractor work was the most fun, and we all eagerly waited until we were old enough to be able to drive the tractor. Driving the tractor was always the privilege of the oldest, while the rest of us had to do the hand labor.

"Dad was a stern taskmaster who demanded that we worked hard and did the job right. Rarely did we receive an encouraging word or a thank you from him for our labors. It was expected that we each carry our own weight with the work to be done. Any shirking resulted in the rest of us having to do more. We usually were able to take care of any shirking by a sibling in our own way. He always was a good example in that he worked hard and set the standard by doing it himself better than we could.

"When I was in high school, I played on the C and B basketball teams my freshman and sophomore years. I was a starter on the C team my freshman year and played as a reserve on the B team as a sophomore. My senior year, as a starter on the varsity team, we had a most successful season, winning the league championship. We went on to win the Valley championship by beating Shafter. I wanted more than anything to play football, but Mom and Dad thought football was a stupid and dangerous sport. I pestered and pleaded my case until finally a family council was held, and all the boys persuaded the folks to let me play my junior and senior years. This required a signature by Dad and also the purchase of special insurance against possible injury. My junior year in high school I was classified as a B player, and being fairly good sized for a B, I played the position of tackle. We had a successful season because we had some juniors and seniors on the team who were not big enough to play on the varsity team who gave good leadership and stability to some of us newcomers.

"My senior year, I was moved to play halfback since I was one of the fastest runners on the team. We had a great season, losing the championship game by two points to San Joaquin Memorial High School from Fresno. I remember with some pride playing against some famous athletes who went on to excel in college and professional football. Rafer Johnson and Monte Clark are two players from Kingsburg High who became well-known athletes beyond high school. Dad began to understand football, and I think he actually enjoyed going to all the home games my senior year.

"I went on to play football at Reedley College for two years and have many fond memories of my playing days. I was honored as an all-conference running back my sophomore year at Reedley College in the Central California Athletic Conference. In those days players played both offense and defense. I played halfback and some fullback on offense, but enjoyed most playing the linebacker position on defense. Being fairly good-sized for a running back, 185 pounds in those days, helped my success.

"Our house on the farm had three bedrooms plus a second-story room underneath the water tank in the tank house and it was surrounded by a screened porch both front and back. Henry and Frank shared the tank-house bedroom while John, myself, and Nick shared a bedroom at the back of the house. At first there was no toilet inside, and we all used the outhouse next to our basketball court. The advent of an indoor toilet was a major accomplishment in our house. I remember helping to dig the pit for the septic tank and also digging the trench for the leachline, which was required for the indoor facilities. Dad did all the plumbing, and we were all very proud of our modern facilities when the project was finished. The house had been built with no concrete foundation to rest on the ground. One of the first major reconstruction projects was to put a foundation under the house. A house-moving outfit jacked it up, and a cement foundation was poured under it. With the house up off the ground, there was room to dig a cellar where canned fruit and other foodstuffs were stored. It was much cooler in the cellar than anywhere else in the house.

"Christmas was always a time eagerly looked forward to by all of us. On Christmas Eve, after coming home from church, we would place a plate on the table with our name attached. Christmas morning we would awake and hurry to the living room to see the goodies, which had been placed at our places. The plate was filled with peanuts and candy. Halva was a special treat we usually found. In addition to the plate full of special things, there also was a gift for each of us. Although I can't remember most of the gifts over the years, there was a truck or toy car for us when we were young enough to cherish those. In my early teens, I re-member getting an electric shaver to shave the fuzz that had begun to grow on my face.

"During high school years, Christmas caroling was a major event. After the Christmas Eve church service, the high school and college age youth would gather at the church and walk around Reedley to sing to the members of the church in their homes. After touring the town, we returned to the church basement for hot chocolate and sandwiches, and then we loaded into cars to travel out of town to carol for the farm families. We usually finished by 2:00 A.M. and returned home to crawl into bed for a short night's sleep. Christmas morning church services were held at 9:00 A.M., and we all were expected to be ready to attend."

My Spiritual Journey

The Bible Institute of Los Angeles was a wonderful place to go to school. After having met the criteria my father had placed on me to allow me to attend high school, I had no problem convincing him of the necessity to continue my education. I knew I had to work my way through school because there was no way that he could help. I was the oldest child, and there were eight others still left at home. He had hoped that I would join the job market and assist him with the family income, but I believe he saw that I was intent on going to school and that I would do my best. My parents took me to the big city of Los Angeles, to the school located on 6th and Hope Street. That was right downtown Los Angeles. They spent one night there at the dormitory and were so overwhelmed with the city that I'm sure they were wondering just how I would manage. They knew also

I was safe in a dormitory, and I believe they trusted God for the rest. They never told me that, but now that I have the benefit of hindsight, I know that this must be true.

To be able to sit under the instruction of godly men and women daily and to live in the dormitory with like-minded people wanting to know God and to learn the Scriptures was the most wonderful experience of my life. I enjoyed every day of those three years, and I have nothing but wonderful memories of that experience. It was a very difficult course of study that I embarked upon. The classroom work required many hours of intense study, and I also had to work. We were allowed to work twenty hours a week, and I did that to pay for my room and board. The faculty was very helpful to me in so many ways. One of the teachers, Miss Nadine Warner, personally worked out a schedule for me because I was failing in a class and I just didn't know what to do. I needed help desperately. I could not fail. She worked with me, and I was able to complete the course with a good grade. Praise God. My major was Bible and Christian Education.

It was at BIOLA where I met Hubert in the India Prayer Band. Ever since I become a Christian, I had a yearning to please God and be involved in full-time missionary work. At BIOLA, I felt a concern for the people of India and I set my heart and goals toward that end. The prayer of my heart was to serve the Lord, and if I did that as a single woman that would be fine, or if the Lord willed to give me a partner with the same vision and goal, I wouldn't mind. So when I met Hubert, I began praying that God's will be done, and we had a four-year courtship relationship that blossomed into marriage and for which I am continually grateful. God gave me a wonderful godly partner.

After graduating from BIOLA, I continued my pursuit of education for the service of God by enrolling at the

Hollywood Presbyterian Hospital School of Nursing. The director of the nursing school program, Miss Ruth Esther Feider, interviewed me, and when I discovered how expensive the tuition was I said to her, "I don't know if I can afford to come here. I am the oldest of nine children, and my parents cannot help me in any way." She replied, "If God wants you here, He will open the way for you." I left her with those words of encouragement, not having any idea of how this was all going to work out.

So the summer between graduation and starting the nursing program, I packed fruit very diligently to earn enough money to get me started in that intensive, three-year (36 months) nursing-education program. God, in His wonderful grace, provided an anonymous benefactor who took care of all of my tuition for that program. All I needed to provide for myself was spending money for my personal needs. I was able to earn that by packing fruit during the two-week break I received each year in the summer.

While I was enrolled in the nursing program, I had a Christian roommate, and God used us in a wonderful way to minister to my classmates and bring them to a saving knowledge of Jesus. We had an ongoing Bible study to help the new Christians grow. God used me and blessed me abundantly in that process. I was able to graduate from the nursing program with top honors. God was faithful to me in that endeavor to prepare myself the best I knew how to serve Him.

Hubert and I were married on October 21, 1949 and we had a large wedding in my hometown. Many of my nursing friends came, including the director of my nursing program, Miss Ruth Esther Feider, who had by that time had acquired one of the highest offices for a nurse in the state of California. She was the executive secretary of the State Board of

Nursing. She was a godly woman and she honored me by being present at my wedding.

My dad was thrilled with my accomplishment, and I was pleased that he was pleased. Both of my parents, of course, were present at my nursing graduation, and I know that Dad was very proud. I had persisted in the quest of getting an education at all costs and it had paid off in immeasurable dividends. We celebrated their silver wedding anniversary at our wedding. It was very special.

Married Love

new chapter in my life begins to unfold. I am now a married woman, married to a wonderful man, and together we wonder how we are going to serve the Lord. We set our hearts together on this and continued to ask God to take charge of our lives and to lead us. We both worked in healthcare fields and became active in our local church. We had established ourselves in a Brethren church in Garvey, California.

Our first two years of marriage saw many changes. We moved several times and we entered several forms of ministry trying to find our way. We had our firstborn son, David, on December 28, 1950. At that time, we were living in a bachelor apartment in the back of a dear friend's home, Herbert and Leona King. They had three boys, and they were very helpful to us. They loved the Lord, and they encouraged us so much. Herb had left a long-time steady job to attend BIOLA and to prepare for the Christian ministry, so we were able to share so much together.

I worked that year at BIOLA, also, as a school nurse. Mrs. King took care of David for me that year.

It was during the next year (1951–52) that Hubert decided that we would go to Winona Lake, Indiana to enroll in the Brethren seminary. I would continue to work at the hospital in Warsaw, Indiana, and he would be in school full-time. We were there several years and then we were given the opportunity to go work among the Navajo Indians in Cuba, New Mexico. We were so thrilled with this wonderful opportunity. We went to the assignment with lots of expectations and with an eagerness that was exciting. My parents had visited us while we were there on the mission compound working, and my dad made the remark, "Well, at last Katharine has found her place, they are so happy in what they are doing, and we are so happy for them." It was just a few weeks after that visit that we were terminated from that assignment. It was very difficult to understand, and we were devastated and crushed. We could not understand at all what the Lord was doing in our lives in causing this terrible disaster—I wept for weeks.

While we were at the mission, I had established a medical clinic, which I held in one small room. I saw pregnant women and made house calls on the sick. I had an immunization program sponsored by the Public Health Department of New Mexico. I established a good liaison with the government hospital at Shiprock and the doctors there. If I had a question about care, they were very willing to help me out in all matters. Hubert and I delivered ten babies in our little clinic and took care of emergencies such as acute illnesses and snakebites. We also helped with the general work of the mission.

We lived in a communal house and ate meals together with others who were working there. Hubert and I had our own bedroom and an additional small room where we had a refrigerator and the crib for David. We were very busy all the time and were looking forward to having permission granted from the home mission board to be allowed to build a house for us to live in. Instead we were terminated. This was very difficult to understand and to deal with. One major learning we experienced was that the grace of God is enough even though we do not understand. He does, and that is enough. In the difficult times, it is good to know that God loves us and comforts us and gives us the ability and strength to trust Him in all things.

New Beginnings

We relocated to Visalia, California, which was between my hometown and Hubert's hometown, to start our lives over. We had spent five years together in earnest, serious preparation only to have all the doors closed to full-time, Christian ministry. So we made the decision to get jobs and to be content in lay ministry, which has been our ministry throughout the years. We are praising God for His continual faithfulness in all our ways.

In the week that we moved to Visalia to start our lives over, Hubert went job hunting, and the very first day, September 13, 1954, he was hired at Sears Roebuck and Company. I got a nursing job at the local hospital working the night shift. Our second son, Jonathan, was born March 5, 1955. We were active in a small mission-Sunday-school and later helped to establish that Sunday school into a thriving church. We purchased our first home in Visalia, and the Lord blessed us with a daughter, Judith Ann, May 18, 1959. What a thrill to have a little girl. I have told her many times that she was the frosting on the cake.

I continued to work nights at the hospital so that I could take care of the children during the day, and Hubert remained at Sears.

My father had a stroke and died in my arms on March 10, 1960. I had made the comment many times that if I did nothing more with my nursing except to take care of my family, that would be enough, and I was able to care for my dad in his dying hours. He was unconscious, and I don't think he was aware of my caring for him, but I was glad to have had that privilege.

We were transferred to the Fullerton Sears Catalog store in 1960, and once again we reestablished ourselves in a good Evangelical Church, the Temple Baptist Church in Fullerton. We became very active in leadership and teaching ministries. I continued to work nights, and I was beginning to get very tired. I only took naps when the children did and was not getting nearly enough sleep. I was becoming more and more discouraged because my life was on a treadmill and I could not get off.

Dr. Bill Bright was invited to our church to share the concepts of Campus Crusade For Christ. We were involved in that seminar. The Lord did a wonderful work in restoration for both of us, and we were renewed in our walk with the Lord. I made a change in my job situation. I had to get off of nights because I was so exhausted and felt only half alive. I could no longer cope with the stresses that were placed on me, so I was offered the job of managing a young new orthopedic surgeon's office. I had learned to know him and the kind of practice he had by working with him in the

Emergency Room at Anaheim Memorial Hospital. I took the job and worked for him for four years, until we were once again transferred, at our request, to the quiet, not so hectic community of Lancaster, California, in 1969. The life in the big city was so stressful that we just had to make a change, and this was going to be the best.

We moved to Lancaster and purchased a lovely home, and I would not have to work any more and life would be wonderful.

Well, my wonderful life of a not working outside of the home lasted approximately six months, and Hubert invited me to consider going back to work. I went to work at the County Facility, which was an acute-alcoholic rehabilitation center as well as a tuberculosis care center. I worked there for one year. I had made application to the local community college for a teaching position in the vocational nursing program. I continued to keep in touch with the director of that program, Mrs. Marian Saunders, so in September of 1971 she asked me to come in for an interview with the academic vice-president, Mr. Jennings Brown. Upon his recommendation to Mr. William Keply, president of the college, I was hired to start teaching immediately in the vocational nursing program. I continued in that role for thirteen years. That was a dream come true.

I had the privilege of enrolling in an extension bachelors degree program out of the University of Redlands and was able to earn the bachelors degree in liberal arts as I continued to work full-time at the Antelope Valley Community College.

I had never imagined in a million years that I would have the good fortune to teach nursing to young, eager students. I loved nursing so much and I wanted to share that love for nursing with others, and I had that privilege. In addition, I have had a big influence in the health care industry in Lancaster by affecting the lives of so many students who graduated from the vocational nursing program and have stayed in the Valley to work.

Those years of teaching were the happiest and most productive years of my life. Of course, if I had not had all the hands-on experiences of the previous twenty-two years in my nursing profession, my teaching would not have been as beneficial as it was. I had actively worked in almost all phases of health care, and so this vast history of my experience served me well.

Hubert and I were active in the local church and served in various capacities. We also continued to hold Bible study, also known as growth groups, in our home. We meet once a week and we have continued that practice for most of the years that we have lived here.

Our oldest son, David, had already graduated from Sunny Hills High school in Fullerton when we moved to Lancaster. He took some classes at the community college and worked in Lancaster for one year and then enlisted in the US Navy and served about eight years. He married my BIOLA roommate's daughter, Carolyn Peterson, in 1972. They have two sons, Michael and James. Michael served in the US Army for four years and is currently employed in North Carolina. James has graduated from high school and is working Reno and plans to continue his education.

Our middle son, Jon, went to Quartz Hill High School here in Lancaster. He was active in student government and athletics. He held the school high-jump record of six feet and six inches for many years. He has two children, Cory, who is now attending college in Montreal and Heidi, who is a graduate of Highland High School and is currently living in Southern California.

Our daughter Judy finished her elementary school and high school education in Quartz Hill. She also was an avid swimmer and swam competitively for about six years and earned All-American swimmer status in 1976. She was the only one to reach that, and at her twentieth high-school reunion in 1997, she still held that distinction.

While they were students in high school, all three of our children rode their bicycles across the United States with the Wandering Wheels Organization out of Upland, Indiana. David crossed coast to coast from Long Beach to Rehoboth Beach, Delaware in 1967. Jon, crossed coast to coast from Cannon Beach, Oregon to Rehoboth Beach, Delaware in 1974, and Judy crossed coast to coast starting at Rehoboth Beach, Delaware to San Diego on our bicentennial celebration in 1976. The trip took six weeks, and they rode their bicycles every mile of the way, averaging approximately 110 miles a day. It was a monumental experience for each of them. Hubert and I were so grateful that they took the opportunity to experience that adventure.

God's Miracle

I n 1977, while attending California State University at Northridge, Judy was involved in a very serious auto accident, which very nearly took her life. It occurred on November 27,1977. It was Thanksgiving weekend and Judy and her roommate and friend, Margaret Sundberg, had come home from school for the weekend. We had missionary visitors in our home and as Judy was leaving to return to school, she said, "Well, goodbye. If I don't see you again in this life, we'll meet in the air."

Our missionary friends, the Burton Clarks, were on their way to Venezuela to continue their missionary service. They had come to visit us before leaving the country. We proceeded to sit down at the table and play a game, and the telephone rang, it was news that there had been an accident involving our Judy and Margaret, and we should go to the scene of the accident on Sierra and L, immediately. When we arrived at the scene, it was a sad sight. Judy was pinned in the vehicle, and the paramedics were already there, working to get her out. She was unconscious, and I was telling the paramedics to ask for Dr. Harvey Birsner to see her. They told us to follow them and inform the hospital on what we wanted to have done. I was in the emergency room with her and saw what was being done in her care to stabilize her. The emergency room doctor told me that Dr.Birsner was out of town and that she would need to be air lifted to UCLA because of her very critical condition.

After an intense conversation with the doctor, I suggested that whoever answered the telephone first, UCLA or Loma Linda Medical Center, would be the place she should go. The emergency room doctor agreed to that proposition. UCLA Medical Center never answered the telephone (they were on strike), and Loma Linda University Medical Center said they would be in the air within twenty minutes. God provided for her to be sent to the Loma Linda medical facility in Redlands, California. She was placed in the neuro intensive care unit. She was in a coma for days. She had bilateral, basal skull fractures and a frontal skull fracture.

We felt so helpless through this strenuous ordeal, but we knew that God was in control. We watched her go down hill day after day and we said, "Lord, You love her more than we do, all we ask is that You accomplish your will through all of this." We did not ask Him to keep her alive. We released her to Him, if He chose to take her home to heaven. We had decided that should the Lord take her home then we would have her organs harvested for someone else to be able to live. When we released her to Him, God began to restore her in a wonderful way. It was not instantaneous. It was a long and tedious process. But, He did restore her completely competent and she continues to bless me in the wonderful miracle that I see every time I speak with her or see her.

To make a long story short, God restored her to us in a wonderful way, and the statement that I usually make when recounting her recovery, "Everything she knows, I taught her twice." She lost her language and she had to relearn all of her skills. She went back to the community college and took remedial work to relearn her basic skills in reading, writing, and mathematics. She graduated with the California Scholarship Federation grades and received the CSF pin on graduation.

She continued on and graduated from Multnomah School of the Bible in Portland, Oregon with a bachelor's degree in biblical studies. She met her husband, Tim Schwab, there and they have four children. Her children are Caleb, Jonathan, Katrina, and Zachary, The story of her miraculous recovery is another long story of the grace and mercy of God in our lives.

29
Retirement

I retired from teaching in 1984. After I retired, I entered into another phase of life that I had always dreamed of. I began ministering to women by teaching women's classes on identifying who they were because of Jesus, not, on their performance. That was a very productive time because I saw so many women transformed in their Christian walk. We also became involved with international students for a month at a time for the benefit of cultural exchange programs, so that they could be absorbed into families and practice conversational English and see first-hand how American families live. Through this program, we have eleven Japanese children. We had the privilege of visiting Japan and stayed with nine families in 1988. What a marvelous opportunity it was to share our lives with these dear people.

Our home has been an open door to all and continues to be so. We love to share our lives and our home with those who come. We praise God for His continual faithfulness to us, in all things and in all ways. Our life is a ministry for Jesus Christ for His Glory and Praise.

Lost in the Mountains

I could experience that peace of God in the midst of the cold and darkness and aloneness of that night. In Psalms 37 verse 23 it says, "The Lord delights in a mans way and he makes his steps firm." He protected me from slipping and falling. He kept me safe from all the lurking danger around me.

We were involved in a four-month program with sixteen Japanese students and five Japanese teachers, staying at a winter ski lodge in Bear Valley, to focus on studying to pass college entrance exams in Japan along with improving their skills in conversational English. We were the directors of that program, providing for their comfort and in meeting the needs of meals and recreation.

On Tuesday June 5, 1990 at 2:00 P.M., we took the class on a nature hike just behind Tamarack Lodge. Hubert and

I had taken the trail before, so I had no reason to fear. I knew the area could be treacherous, but since we had taken the trail, I was confident that there would be no problem. I did not anticipate the students attitude and non-interest in this activity. Two of the girls had just asked permission to leave the pack and return home because the mosquitoes were bothering them. I told them no because they would get lost, but they went home anyhow (Which was the best choice they made, I have since decided). However, four of the boys held way back, and I had just shown one of the boys a pine nut and how to find them. He seemed more interested in finding some of the other items on the list. The four boys decided they would not continue on the trail. I had just turned off to look at a little stream to see if I could see a fish and then I continued to follow in their direction. I did not want to cross the marshy meadow because it was so very wet. I crossed the area on a little dryer spot and it was there that I made a wrong turn. At any rate, I was lost. Totally and completely lost. The trail did not take me to Tamarack as I had expected, but into the forest. I prayed and asked the Lord to show me the way out and to safety. I walked until 8:00 P.M., when it got to dark to continue. I walked toward Bear Valley thinking I could at least get to highway # 4. I climbed many large boulders and cliffs, always trying to be as visible as possible because by the time it was 7:00 P.M. I felt that Hubert would have realized that I was lost and perhaps there would be a search and rescue team out looking for me. I continued to ask the Lord for wisdom. It seemed like I was in a nightmare and that I would wake up anytime knowing it was just in a dream. That, of course, was not so.

I crossed several streams thinking that if I crossed them and headed in what I thought to be west, I would get to the highway. When I finally reached the Bear Valley end, I looked over that direction and I thought I saw buildings that could have been part of Bear Valley. There was no way I could get down the cliffs and boulders to the road to that area. It was much too dangerous and still not a sure thing. Because it was getting later and later, I felt my next decision was to find a place for shelter for the night. I knew by now that I probably would not be found until daylight and perhaps no one was looking because it was nightfall. I still wanted to be visible just in case they would be looking for me. I decided to lean against a big rock that had some pine needles on the base of it that would be good for a pillow. I put my keys into my pocket so I wouldn't loose them and I pulled my sweater over my head because the mosquitoes were terrible. The biting never stopped. I pulled my arms in close to my body inside the sweater and sat leaning against the rock trying to get some sleep. I was so exhausted from walking from 2:00 P.M. that I must have fallen asleep. Then I awakened at 11:00 P.M., the moon was very bright. I could read my watch and I thanked the Lord for His sovereign will, even though I could not understand any of this. I also felt so foolish for having gotten lost, although I had not been foolish in the walk. I just could not fathom how this could have happened. I still felt like this was a bad dream.

I kept listening for search dogs and people but heard nothing. It was getting very cold and I laid down and curled up and tried to sleep. I shivered. I kept awaking every hour or so shivering. My sleep was not restful at all. My joints were beginning to ache and the pain was almost unbearable. My legs cramped so severely that I hardly knew what to do. I was unable to walk because of the pain, so I would gently stretch my legs out and lie very still hoping the cramp would go away.

At 4:00 A.M., once again, I was surveying the sky. The moon was now being covered by a cloud, and the sky seemed to be cloudy all over, and it was getting colder and colder. I shivered almost constantly now. I was desperately waiting for 5:00 A.M. so that I would be able to see well enough to walk again. I talked to the Lord about my situation and that I was desperate and unable to get myself out of this lost situation. I asked the Lord to please show me, to guide my feet as I couldn't hear his voice, but to please direct me so that I would understand which way to go to get to the road so that I could find my way back to camp again. I thanked the Lord for His sovereign will and asked Him to reassure Hubert of my safety and to give guidance to those who might me looking for me. I could not understand why I had not heard anything or anyone or any barking dogs. I knew that Bear Valley and Calaveras County had a very good search and rescue team, but I was wondering why I had not been found. For a while, it looked like it was going to snow, and I pleaded with the Lord to stop the storm. I would not be able to survive a storm like that because I would be totally lost in the snow and I was not dressed for that kind of weather and the exposure would be too much. Never the less, the Lord's will be done.

When morning came, I once again began walking. I kept looking for a trail. I walked in areas I had not walked the day before. Those sections all looked so different, and I very carefully looked at each possibility. I finally took one trail that I had not been on and looked toward what I thought was west and I thought I saw a road or a reflection of a road. I also thought I heard a car, so I walked in that direction. I came onto a rushing stream, but very swift and it had many big boulders in it. I found a group of boulders that I thought I could cross if I crawled across them rather than try to jump them. I was very fearful of falling and slipping on the wet boulders and being badly hurt out there alone. I safely crossed the stream and headed in the direction where I thought I had seen the road. There I found a huge corral that was empty and an old abandoned building. A very tight, barbed wire fence surrounded this area. I crawled under it and followed the roadway to the highway that I thought was highway # 4. (At least it was a paved road.) I started walking, knowing I would have all day, if need be, to walk that highway and find out where I was.

After walking past three or four curves, a vehicle approached, which I thought was a station wagon, and I saw a man driving the car, and I flagged him down with my clipboard. He slowed down and I told him I was lost. He said, "Are you Katharine?" I told him yes, and he said, "Thank God you are safe. We have been looking for you all night." He called the base at Tamarack and told them he had found me and was bringing me in. I could not contain my tears any longer. I had not allowed myself to cry at anytime while I was trying to find my way. I knew I had to keep it all together to survive the elements and the walking.

When I arrived at Tamarack there were many trucks, many uniformed men in yellow slickers, all kinds of people in the search party. The lodge had become the headquarters, and these men had taken different areas all night. They would not allow Hubert to join in the search because they did not want my tracks to be disturbed. When I fell into Huberts arms, I wept and wept. Sally Anderson, the bosses wife, also was there. She had been doing her share of weeping because the men could not determine why I was not hearing them. They felt that perhaps I had been injured somewhere and was not able to hear them. They had gotten the search dogs early in the morning, and the dogs had picked up my scent and where I walked out. They were fifteen minutes behind me. The helicopters had been ordered, but when I was found they were canceled. Walter Anderson, the boss, said later, "You could have delayed walking out for about fifteen minutes to at least build my ego up." Everyone was happy to see me safe, of course, and no happier than I was. The students and staff had been up all night worried and concerned. Diane, the cook, had been cooking for the men all night. Everyone worked very hard to locate me. How thankful I am that so many people cared. Hubert called our children after I was safe. He did not call them before because he would not have been able to handle it at that time and there was no reason to get them upset before he knew the outcome.

I was not ever fearful. I was concerned about finding my way out or being found. I was able to rest in the sovereignty of God and knew that He knew where I was and would accomplish His will in all of this. I asked Him to show me the way out and He did in a wonderful way. God is so good.

I was totally exhausted. I was so cold and shivered so hard all that night that I had not been able to get over the exhaustion. It took me more than a week to recuperate. I was amazed at how thorough the search and rescue team had been. They had found my tracks all over the place and they had been able to track me quite well. I was so glad to hear that they even knew which boulders I had climbed over and which ones I had gone around. I am very much amazed how skilled those men were and how well they organized the team to do the search effectively and to conserve as much human energy as possible.

I was able to share the absence of fear with the students because God is faithful.

31 In Conclusion

As I have reflected over the past several years, (the time it has taken to review the history and to write what I could remember and what I have been told), I am always so amazed at the sovereignty of God in all things and especially as related to the affairs of our family's lives and sojourns.

In May of 1997, my sister Helen and I had the opportunity to visit Germany and to visit relatives of my dad that we had never met and also of my mother that we had not had the privilege of meeting before. They had all immigrated into Germany in recent years, and now we have had the opportunity to visit with them and to find out what had happened in this sixty-five year interim from when we left Russia in 1929 until 1997.

Let me back up just a bit. Two years prior, we had a very special, unique thing happen. My brother Nick received a phone call from another relative who had seen our family picture taken in 1937 in a German publication called the *Mennonitshe Bote*. Under the picture was the request that if anyone knew of the whereabouts of our family to please call a number in Germany. My brother Nick telephoned my sister Helen, and she told him to call me because I would know what to do. As soon as I received this information, I telephoned the number in Germany and identified myself. The person on the other end was so overwhelmed that a response had come from the ad they had placed in the *Bote*. That conversation led to identification that she was my father's sister's daughter and therefore, my father was her uncle. We had thought that all of the family had perished in the late thirty's, during the great famine and Stalin's purge.

The following summer, June 1996, the family came to visit us here in California, and we had a wonderful time becoming acquainted with Vilmar and Katya Tessman. They were able to meet all of us nine brothers and sisters in California, and what a thrill that was. As a result of that reunion, my sister and I went to Germany in May of 1997 to meet others of the family that we had not met before. We spent fourteen days in Germany and visited with many family members and asked many questions. We received some answers, but the upper most thought in our minds was, *My, the grace of God in our lives.* How thankful we continued to be that our parents had the courage in their young lives to pull up stakes and leave their country and venture into an unknown world. I was more and more impressed with the knowledge that my father was only thirty years old and my mother twenty-seven years old with three small children with the fourth baby on the way to take the risk of traveling to a foreign country and to start a new life without any guarantees. How I praise God for this.

We had two weeks of visiting with those relatives and comparing experiences, weeping together, and laughing together. One day my sister and I were sitting around the kitchen table visiting with Katya, my father's niece, and Elena, my mothers niece, and her daughters, Katya, Elwira, and Emma, my mothers grand nieces. We were together sharing for the first time in sixty-five years and we were communicating in our mother's tongue. I was so overwhelmed at the miracle of all of this. It is beyond explanation.

Their lives were riddled with sadness and sorrow over what they had experienced in Russia after we left. They were raised in communist Russia with the communist dogma and have no understanding, as it were, of the spiritual truth that has been my privilege to embrace. They kept telling us it had been against the law to have any access or exposure to the Scriptures or its teachings. All they had was what they had heard at their grandmothers knees. They have no knowledge of a personal relational God. They believe in God as the Creator, but do not know Him in a personal way. They continued to ask where was God when they needed Him?

As we came to learn later, in the years of 1937–38 there had not been enough food to feed all of the people in the prison labor-camp. The prisoners went on strike. If they would not be fed they would not work, and during this time, a purging of the camps occurred. We believe that Peter was executed at that time. The reason that he was taken as prisoner in the first place was because he was accused of having received letters from relatives in the US. That is why Peter Block II, the son of the banished Peter, instructed my parents via his wife, not to ever write to him. He did not wish to receive any correspondence from the United States under any circumstances. The mail could be sent to his sisters' homes or other relatives. He always delivered the mail to the relatives and he kept very close watch on correspondence and kept a tight reign on any activities the relatives were involved in because he was not going to let what had happened to his father happen to him. That is why he was so strict with all of the family members. He wept every time he read or had the letters read to him.

Peter II became a communist party member and had a good job. They did not require military service from him because he was the oldest son and he had the responsibility of the younger siblings Jacob, Lena, and Tina as well as his mother. His mother died of a broken heart six years later. The youngest daughter, Tina, was twelve years old. She was only six when we left. Peter had to care for her until she got married. After Tina was married, she would be on her own. She took her own life. She left behind a family of five children and she had a good husband. No one knew why she took her own life.

That has been very hard on Lena. Every letter she writes she brings up the issue of not ever being able to see her sister again. They did not let her go to her own mother's funeral when she died. She was only sixteen years. old. Jacob, her brother, was in a different labor camp than she was and they let him go home but not her.

During my visit with her in Germany in May of 1997, she related to me the facts and details of Tina's death and other tragedies of her life during those years. In 1982 Peter Block II took his wife's life and his own. That was followed by Lena's son, Peter, who was an identical twin to Victor, taking his own life at age twenty-eight in 1985. Jacob, the other brother to Lena, died of a fibrous lung disease in 1984.

We also had met Jacob and visited with him in 1978. Then in 1991, Paul, Lena's husband, died of cancer after a lengthy illness. So Lena is the only member of my mother's family left abroad. Lena has a number of children whom we met in Germany on our visit in May of 1997. The children of Peter Block II still live in Russia. I have met the son Jacob when he visited us here in California in the fall of 1995 and have spoken with Anna, the daughter, on the telephone. She also still lives in Russia with her husband.

My sister and I kept saying, "But for the grace of God this would be our plight." We thank God we know that our salvation is secure in Christ Jesus and He has redeemed us and we are called by His name. We have peace with God and the peace of God is dwelling in our hearts and lives. That is the reason I have felt compelled to write this account of the faithfulness of God to our family and to give Him praise and honor. So that our younger generations coming up after us will know the leading, protection, and guidance of God our Heavenly Father in our lives and His leading us from a land of despair (Russia) into the land of deliverance (California) and the United States of America.

Bibliography

H.P. Isaak, *Our Life Story and Escape*, 1977

John Block, *Escape Siberia to California*, 1995

Norma Jost Voth, *Mennonite Foods & Folkways from South Russia*, Volumes 1 & 2 (Intercourse, PA: Good Books, 1990)

Michael Phillips /Judith Pella, *The Russians Series,* Vol 1–3 (Minneapolis: Bethany House, 1992)

Judith Pella, *The Russians Series,* Vol 4–7 (Minneapolis: Bethany House, 1998)

Dr. Walter Quiring /Helen Bartel, *In the Fullness of Time: 150 years of Mennonite Sojourn in Russia* (Kitchener, Onario: Aron Klassen, 1974)

To order additional copies of

From Despair
to Deliverance

send $11.99 plus $3.95 shipping and handling to

Books Etc.
PO Box 4888
Seattle, WA 98104

or have your credit card ready and call

(800) 917-BOOK

Our last family picture with our Mother in 1989. Back row: Frank, Peter, Henry, John, and Nick Rogalsky. Seated: Ann, Katharine, Mother, Helen, and Mary.

Helen (Rogalsky) Pauls. Children: Roger Pauls, Daryl & Kimber Pauls, Karen & David Anderson.

Dr. Warren & Anna (Rogalsky) Simon. Children: Barbara and Buck Uhlman, Ralph (deceased) & Linda Simon, Carol & Jeff Townsend, Janet & Oscar Galindo.

Dr. Alvin & Mary (Rogalsky) Nickel. Children: Jeff & Cindy Nickel, Bob & Susanne Nickel, Cathy & Jim Harris.

Dr. Peter & Virginia Rogalsky. Children: Peter & Kristianne Rogalsky, Tom & Cheryle Evans Rogalsky, Julie & Abe Gueller.

Nick & Grace Rogalsky. Children: Shelly and Dave Sorenson, Debbie & Rick Linman.

John & Frances Rogalsky. Children: Scott & Kelly Rogalsky, Peggy & Jim Foster, Cheryl & Greg Brand, Ann & Randy Guerrero.

Henry & Kathryn Rogalsky. Children: Sue
& Sam Frantz, Janice & Larry Maaske.

Frank and Ruth Rogalsky. Children:
Ron and Crystal Rogalsky, Linda and
Patrick Stevens.

Kathrine (Rogalsky)
& Hubert Sylvester.
Children: David Leonard
& Carolyn Sylvester,
Jonathan Paul Sylvester,
Judith Ann Schwab.

Dad's nephews Abram Tows, Johann Tows, and his niece Katya Tessman.

Taken May 1997 during a visit to Germany with my sister. This was the first family reunion in 65 years.

Front row: Katya Tessman, Elena Obgolz, Katya Barbie, Katya Obgolz, Helen Pauls, and Vilmer Tessman. Back row: Victor Olgoz, Katharine Sylvester, Alexander Kaist, and Elwira Kaist.